QUICK
FAMILY MEALS

This book is published in 2014 by Bounty Books based on materials licensed to it by Bauer Media Books, Sydney

Bauer Media Books are published by
Bauer Media Limited 54 Park St, Sydney

GPO Box 4088, Sydney, NSW 2001.

phone (02) 9282 8618; fax (02) 9126 3702

www.awwcookbooks.com.au

BAUER MEDIA BOOKS

Publisher – Sally Wright

Editorial & Food Director – Pamela Clark

Director of Sales, Marketing & Rights – Brian Cearnes

Creative Director – Hieu Chi Nguyen

Printed in China by 1010 Printing Asia Limited.

Published and Distributed in the United Kingdom by Octopus Publishing Group

Endeavour House

189 Shaftesbury Avenue

London WC2H 8JY

United Kingdom

phone (+44)(0)207 632 5400; fax (+44)(0)207 632 5405

info@octopus-publishing.co.uk;

www.octopusbooks.co.uk

International foreign language rights,
Brian Cearnes, Bauer Media Books
bcearnes@bauer-media.com.au

A catalogue record for this book is available from the British Library.

ISBN: 978-0-75372-693-8

THE AUSTRALIAN
Women's Weekly

QUICK
FAMILY MEALS

BB **Bounty**
BOOKS

contents

Eating as a family

The value of a family meal enjoyed around the dining room table is something everyone can agree on, but, as we've all heard before, we're becoming increasingly time-poor and are often too busy to enjoy the lighter side of life.

While sitting down together to share the day's events over a home cooked meal may seem like a bit of a luxury, it encourages healthy eating and spending time with our loved ones. This sets an important example for our children, as the habits we form in childhood and adolescence affect our behaviour in later life.

It's hard to ignore these benefits so, rather than simply 'making time', let's find ways to make the most of the limited time we have.

Get Organised

The key to making the most of your time is organisation. A simple first step is to sit down on the weekend to plan the week's meals. Then you can make a shopping list and stock up on everything you'll need.

Having a well-organised kitchen with common utensils within easy reach assists your cooking efforts. Make sure knives, vegetable peelers and graters are sharp – blunt blades are dangerous and can be frustrating especially when you're in a rush.

Read the whole recipe in advance so you know what to expect: do you need the oven heated? Do you need boiling water? Do you need a piece of specialist equipment? These tips will help you beat the clock.

Prepare Ahead

Lack of preparation is where it's easiest to come unstuck, but some simple tricks can save time.

Pre-packaged products from supermarkets are tasty shortcuts to preparing meals. Try salad mixes, peeled and pre-cut vegetables, barbecued chickens, stir-fry mixes, pasta sauces, curry pastes, pizza bases, marinades, salad dressings and frozen pastry.

Butchers have a handy range of trimmed, sliced, diced, marinated, crumbed and skewered meats that save time and effort. With the hard work done, all that's left is to weigh and measure everything before starting to cook the recipe.

Family Favourites

Quick Family Meals isn't just about getting dinner on the table in a hurry; these meals are also balanced and nutritious. And all our recipes have been tested three times to ensure that the timing is spot on, so everything should be on the table in 40 minutes or less. Importantly though, we haven't sacrificed flavour for speed. Fresh is just as important as fast!

You may find that you are slower when you first start, but don't let this stop you. The more you cook, the faster you will become. With practice, you will feel confident to try something different, and you may just discover your family's new favourite meal.

one pot

What could be easier than cooking dinner all in the same pot? One-pot cooking enhances flavour and reduces washing up.

pork sausage and lentil stew

16 pork chipolata sausages (680g)

cooking-oil spray

2 teaspoons fennel seeds

⅓ cup (80ml) dry red wine

400g (12½ ounces) canned diced tomatoes

400g (12½ ounces) canned brown lentils, rinsed, drained

½ cup (100g) drained char-grilled capsicum
(bell pepper), sliced thinly

⅓ cup shredded fresh basil leaves

2 tablespoons extra virgin olive oil

1 Pierce each chipolata once. Spray a large saucepan with oil; cook chipolatas over high heat, in batches, for 5 minutes or until browned all over.

2 Return sausages to pan, add seeds; cook, stirring, over medium heat, for 1 minute or until fragrant. Stir in wine, tomatoes, lentils and capsicum; bring to the boil. Simmer, covered, for 5 minutes or until sausages are cooked through and sauce has thickened slightly. Stir in half the basil; season to taste.

3 To serve, drizzle stew with oil and top with remaining basil.

prep + cook time 15 minutes **serves** 4
nutritional count per serving 60.5g total fat
(22.2g saturated fat); 3210kJ (767 cal);
17.5g carbohydrate; 33.5g protein; 7.7g fibre

serving suggestion Crusty bread and mashed potato.

tips You can use cannellini or small lima beans for the white beans. Soup can be kept refrigerated for 2 days or frozen for 2 months. Add a little extra stock or water when reheating if the soup has thickened.

white bean and chickpea soup with risoni

1 tablespoon olive oil

1 medium brown onion (150g), chopped coarsely

1 large carrot (180g), chopped coarsely

2 cloves garlic, sliced thinly

2 tablespoons tomato paste

2 teaspoons ground cumin

800g (1½ pounds) canned crushed tomatoes

1 litre (4 cups) vegetable stock

400g (12½ ounces) canned chickpeas (garbanzo beans), rinsed, drained

400g (12½ ounces) canned white beans, rinsed, drained

⅓ cup (75g) risoni

1 Heat oil in a large saucepan over medium-high heat; cook onion and carrot, stirring, for 5 minutes or until carrot softens. Add garlic, paste and cumin; cook, stirring, until garlic softens.
2 Add tomatoes and stock to pan; bring to the boil. Add chickpeas and beans; return to the boil. Add risoni; boil, uncovered, for 10 minutes or until risoni is tender. Season to taste.

prep + cook time 30 minutes **serves** 4
nutritional count per serving 7.8g total fat (1.4g saturated fat); 1359kJ (325 cal); 41.9g carbohydrate; 15.5g protein; 11.6g fibre

chilli con carne with quesadillas

1 tablespoon olive oil

300g (9½ ounces) minced (ground) beef

1 medium red onion (170g), chopped finely

2 cloves garlic, crushed

1 tablespoon worcestershire sauce

1 tablespoon Tabasco sauce

2 teaspoons each ground cumin and coriander

1 teaspoon dried oregano

400g (12½ ounces) canned crushed tomatoes

½ cup (130g) chunky tomato salsa

400g (12½ ounces) canned kidney beans, rinsed, drained

400g (12½ ounces) canned chickpeas (garbanzo beans), rinsed, drained

quesadillas

¾ cup (90g) coarsely grated cheddar

4 x 20cm (8-inch) flour tortillas

20g (¾ ounce) butter, softened

1 Heat half the oil in a medium saucepan over medium-high heat; cook beef, stirring, until browned. Remove from pan. Heat remaining oil in same pan; cook onion and garlic, stirring, for 5 minutes until onion softens. Return beef to pan with sauces, cumin, coriander and oregano; cook, stirring, for 2 minutes.
2 Add tomatoes then salsa, beans and chickpeas to pan; simmer, uncovered, for 10 minutes or until thickened. Season to taste.
3 Meanwhile, make quesadillas. Serve chilli with quesadillas.

quesadillas Divide the cheddar between two tortillas; top with remaining tortillas, pressing firmly to seal. Brush tortillas lightly with butter. Cook separately in a heated sandwich press until browned and cheese is melted. Cut each quesadilla into quarters.

prep + cook time 35 minutes **serves** 4
nutritional count per serving 26.8g total fat
(11.1g saturated fat); 2562kJ (613 cal);
51.7g carbohydrate; 35.5g protein; 11.6g fibre

tips If you have some, add ⅓ cup loosely packed fresh coriander leaves (cilantro) to the chilli con carne just before serving. Chilli can be refrigerated for up to 2 days or frozen for up to 2 months. Add a little water when reheating if the chilli has thickened. You can also cook the quesadillas in a frying pan. To save time, serve the chilli with heated microwavable white or brown rice instead of quesadillas.

tips Jalapeño chillies are found in jars, sliced and pickled in brine, in the condiment or Mexican food aisle in most supermarkets. They are quite hot. The pork mixture can be made a day ahead.

pork and bean burritos

1 tablespoon olive oil

½ small brown onion (40g), chopped finely

2 teaspoons each ground cumin, coriander and smoked paprika

1 tablespoon finely chopped fresh coriander (cilantro) root and stem

2 teaspoons bottled crushed garlic

500g (1 pound) minced (ground) pork

200g (6½ ounces) canned cherry tomatoes

8 x 20cm (8-inch) flour tortillas

450g (14½ ounces) microwavable white long-grain rice

400g (12½ ounces) canned mexican beans

½ cup loosely packed fresh coriander leaves (cilantro)

⅔ cup (80g) coarsely grated cheddar

⅔ cup (160g) sour cream

1 medium lime (90g)

⅓ cup (80g) drained pickled jalapeño chillies, optional

1 Heat oil in a large frying pan over high heat.

2 Cook onion, spices, coriander root and stem mixture and garlic, stirring, until onion softens. Add pork; cook, stirring, until browned. Add canned tomatoes; cook, stirring, for 5 minutes or until thick. Season to taste.

3 Meanwhile, microwave tortillas and rice, separately, according to packet directions. Microwave beans until heated, then toss through the rice.

4 Top tortillas with pork mixture, rice mixture, coriander leaves, cheddar and sour cream. Remove rind from lime with a zester (or slice rind very thinly); sprinkle on top with the chilli.

prep + cook time 25 minutes **makes** 8
nutritional count per burrito 20.9g total fat
(9.8g saturated fat); 1877kJ (449 cal);
40.1g carbohydrate; 22.7g protein; 4.6g fibre

tip With a name that loosely translates as 'top of the shop', ras el hanout is a Moroccan blend of the very best spices that a spice merchant has to offer: allspice, cumin, paprika, fennel, caraway and saffron are all generally part of the mix.

moroccan beef couscous

2 tablespoons olive oil

4 x 220g (7-ounce) new-york cut steaks

1 tablespoon ras el hanout

1 tablespoon finely grated lemon rind

⅓ cup (80ml) lemon juice

⅔ cup (160ml) dry white wine

1 cup (250ml) water

1 small red onion (100g), chopped finely

2 cups (400g) couscous

½ cup coarsely chopped fresh mint

¼ cup coarsely chopped fresh flat-leaf parsley

¼ cup (50g) toasted pepitas

⅓ cup (95g) yoghurt

lemon cheeks or wedges, to serve

1 Heat oil in a large deep frying pan over medium-high heat; rub beef with ras el hanout. Cook beef, uncovered, until cooked as desired, turning once only. Remove from pan; rest, covered, for 5 minutes, then slice thinly.

2 Wipe pan clean, then add rind, juice, wine and the water to pan; cover, bring to the boil then remove from heat. Add onion and couscous to pan; cover, stand for 5 minutes or until liquid is absorbed, fluffing with fork occasionally. Stir in herbs and pepitas. Season to taste.

3 Serve couscous topped with steak and drizzled with yoghurt; accompany with lemon cheeks.

prep + cook time 20 minutes **serves** 4
nutritional count per serving 29.6g total fat (8.5g saturated fat); 3687kJ (882 cal); 82.3g carbohydrate; 64.3g protein; 2.5g fibre

tips Diced vegetable soup mix contains chopped carrot, onion and celery. It can be found in the chilled lettuce section of major supermarkets. Soup can be kept refrigerated for up to 2 days or frozen for up to 2 months. Add a little extra stock or water when reheating if the soup has thickened.

bacon, vegetable and lentil soup

1 tablespoon olive oil

400g (12½-ounce) packet diced fresh vegetable soup mix

2 cloves garlic, crushed

3 rindless bacon slices (195g), chopped finely

1 cup (200g) dried red lentils

1 litre (4 cups) salt-reduced chicken stock

2 tablespoons coarsely chopped fresh chives

2 tablespoons coarsely chopped fresh flat-leaf parsley

1 tablespoon finely chopped fresh tarragon

1 Heat oil in a large saucepan over high heat; add soup mix, garlic and bacon. Cook, stirring, for 5 minutes or until vegetables soften.
2 Add lentils and stock; bring to the boil. Simmer, uncovered, stirring occasionally, for 15 minutes or until lentils are tender and soup has thickened. Season to taste.
3 Serve soup sprinkled with herbs; accompany with fresh crusty bread rolls, if you like.

prep + cook time 30 minutes **serves** 4
nutritional count per serving 13.4g total fat
(3.6g saturated fat); 1417kJ (338 cal);
26g carbohydrate; 24.9g protein; 10.2g fibre

chorizo stew

300g (9½ ounces) small kipfler (fingerling) potatoes

2 tablespoons olive oil

2 cured chorizo sausages (340g), sliced thinly

1 medium red onion (170g), sliced thickly

1 large red capsicum (bell pepper) (350g), sliced thickly

1 large yellow capsicum (bell pepper) (350g), sliced thickly

1 teaspoon each ground cumin, coriander and smoked paprika

3 cloves garlic, sliced thinly

2 dried bay leaves

1 cup (250ml) chicken stock

800g (1½ pounds) canned cherry tomatoes

¼ cup loosely packed fresh flat-leaf parsley leaves

1 loaf sliced sourdough bread (450g)

1 tablespoon olive oil

1 tablespoon bottled crushed garlic

2 tablespoons finely chopped fresh flat-leaf parsley

1 Scrub potatoes; dry. Place in a medium microwave-safe bowl, cover; microwave on HIGH (100%) for 3 minutes or until almost tender. Cover to keep warm.

2 Meanwhile, heat oil in a medium saucepan over high heat; cook chorizo, onion, capsicum and spices, stirring, for 5 minutes or until chorizo is browned and onion softens. Add garlic and bay leaves; cook, stirring, for 1 minute.

3 Slice potatoes into thick rounds. Add potato, stock and tomatoes to pan; bring to the boil. Reduce heat; simmer, covered, 3 minutes or until vegetables are tender. Season to taste. Sprinkle with parsley leaves.

4 Preheat grill (broiler). Toast bread. Combine oil, crushed garlic and chopped parsley in a small bowl; brush over one side of toast. Serve toast with stew.

prep + cook time 15 minutes serves 4
nutritional count per serving 41.1g total fat
(11.3g saturated fat); 3412kJ (815 cal);
77.1g carbohydrate; 27.4g protein; 13g fibre

pasta

fettuccine with tomato and rocket pesto

Cook 500g (1lb) fettuccine in a large saucepan of boiling water until tender; drain. Make rocket pesto by blending 8 garlic cloves, ½ cup coarsely chopped fresh basil, 120g (4oz) coarsely chopped rocket leaves and ⅔ cup olive oil until smooth. Quarter a 250g (8oz) punnet truss roma (egg) tomatoes. Combine pasta, pesto, ½ cup finely grated parmesan, tomato, 2 tablespoons lemon juice and 2 thinly sliced fresh small red thai (serrano) chillies in a large saucepan; stir over medium heat until hot. Add ⅓ cup toasted pine nuts; toss gently to combine.

prep + cook time 25 minutes **serves** 4
nutritional count per serving 50.1g total fat (8g saturated fat); 3779kJ (904 cal); 88.9g carbohydrate; 21.1g protein; 7.3g fibre

spaghetti with pesto

Cook 375g (12oz) spaghetti in a large saucepan of boiling water until tender; drain. Meanwhile, blend or process 2 cups coarsely chopped fresh basil, 2 tablespoons roasted pine nuts and 2 cloves garlic until smooth. With processor operating, add ⅓ cup olive oil in a thin steady stream; process until mixture is combined. Place pesto in a medium bowl; stir in ¼ cup grated parmesan. Combine pasta with pesto in a large bowl; toss gently. Serve with flakes of parmesan, if you like.

prep + cook time 30 minutes **serves** 4
nutritional count per serving 26g total fat (4.1g saturated fat); 2328kJ (557 cal); 65g carbohydrate; 13.7g protein; 4.3g fibre

fettuccine carbonara

Cook 500g (1lb) fettuccine in a large saucepan of boiling water until tender; drain. Return pasta to pan; cover to keep warm. Meanwhile, cook 6 thinly sliced rindless bacon rashers in a large frying pan, stirring, until crisp. Add 100g (3oz) thinly sliced button mushrooms; cook, stirring, until tender. Add 300ml pouring cream; stir until heated through. Combine 4 lightly beaten eggs and 1 cup coarsely grated parmesan in a small bowl. Working quickly, gently combine bacon mixture, hot pasta and combined egg and cheese. Serve topped with fresh parsley leaves, if you like.

prep + cook time 20 minutes **serves** 4
nutritional count per serving 57.6g total fat (31.9g saturated fat); 3407kJ (815 cal); 33.5g carbohydrate; 40.4g protein; 2.9g fibre

smoked salmon, fennel and dill pasta

Cook 250g (8oz) linguine pasta in a large saucepan of boiling water until tender; drain. Rinse under cold water; drain. Place pasta in a large bowl with 2 trimmed, thinly sliced small fennel bulbs, 1 thinly sliced medium red onion, 200g (6½oz) thinly sliced smoked salmon, ¼ cup rinsed, drained, coarsely chopped capers, ½ cup loosely packed fresh dill and ½ cup crème fraîche; toss gently. Combine 2 teaspoons finely grated lemon rind and ¼ cup lemon juice, add to pasta; toss gently to combine.

prep + cook time 25 minutes **serves** 4
nutritional count per serving 15.2g total fat (8.5g saturated fat); 1777kJ (425 cal); 49g carbohydrate; 20.5g protein; 4.4g fibre

beef and bean tostadas with chunky guacamole

6 x 15cm (6-inch) corn tortillas

cooking-oil spray

1 tablespoon olive oil

1 medium red onion (170g), chopped finely

300g (9½ ounces) minced (ground) beef

400g (12½ ounces) canned red kidney beans, rinsed, drained

1½ cups (400g) mild taco sauce

1 medium avocado (250g)

⅓ cup loosely packed coriander leaves (cilantro)

1 tablespoon lime juice

150g (4½ ounces) sour cream

lime cheeks or wedges, to serve

1 Preheat oven to 200°C/400°F.

2 Microwave tortillas according to directions on packet. Spray tortillas on both sides with oil; press into holes of a 6-hole (¾-cup/180ml) texas muffin pan. Bake for 8 minutes or until browned lightly.

3 Meanwhile, heat olive oil in a large frying pan over high heat; cook three-quarters of the onion, stirring, until softened. Add beef; cook, stirring, until browned. Add beans and taco sauce to pan. Simmer, uncovered, for 3 minutes or until thick. Season to taste.

4 To make guacamole, peel and coarsely mash avocado in a small bowl with a fork; stir in remaining onion, coriander and juice. Season to taste.

5 Divide beef mixture into tortillas; top with guacamole. Serve with sour cream and lime cheeks, if you like.

prep + cook time 25 minutes **makes** 6
nutritional count per tostada 24.4g total fat
(10.1g saturated fat); 1555kJ (371 cal);
19.1g carbohydrate; 16.1g protein; 6.4g fibre

serving suggestion Leafy green salad.

meatballs in spicy coconut milk

800g (1½ pounds) minced (ground) beef

2 eggs

2 teaspoons cornflour (cornstarch)

2 cloves garlic, crushed

1 tablespoon finely chopped fresh coriander (cilantro)

1 fresh long red chilli, chopped finely

2 purple shallots (50g), chopped coarsely

3 cloves garlic, extra, quartered

1 teaspoon chilli flakes

7 fresh long red chillies, extra, chopped coarsely

2 tablespoons peanut oil

10g (½ ounce) fresh galangal, sliced thinly

3 large tomatoes (660g), seeded, chopped coarsely

1⅔ cups (400ml) canned coconut milk

1 tablespoon kecap asin

1 large tomato (220g), extra, seeded, diced

½ cup (40g) fried shallots

1 fresh small red thai (serrano) chilli, sliced thinly

1 Combine beef, eggs, cornflour, crushed garlic, coriander and finely chopped chilli in a medium bowl; roll level tablespoons of mixture into balls. Place meatballs, in a single layer, in a large baking-paper-lined bamboo steamer. Steam, covered, over a wok of simmering water for 10 minutes.

2 Meanwhile, blend or process purple shallots, quartered garlic, chilli flakes, coarsely chopped chilli and half the oil until mixture forms a paste.

3 Heat remaining oil in a wok; cook shallot paste and galangal, stirring, for 1 minute or until fragrant. Add chopped tomato; cook, stirring, for 1 minute. Add coconut milk, kecap asin and meatballs; simmer, uncovered, stirring occasionally, for 5 minutes or until meatballs are cooked through and sauce thickens slightly. Season to taste.

4 Serve curry topped with diced tomato, fried shallots and thinly sliced chilli.

prep + cook time 40 minutes **serves** 4
nutritional count per serving 47.1g total fat
(26.5g saturated fat); 2721kJ (651 cal);
8.3g carbohydrate; 47.7g protein; 3.9g fibre

tips This recipe showcases the significant influences on Singaporean cooking by its near neighbours – borrowing culinary techniques from Malaysia, India and China, chillies and spices laced with coconut milk are a characteristic of this island nation's cuisine. The recipe can be made a day ahead to the end of step 2; keep refrigerated.

tips Cauliflower is a popular choice for vegetarian curries because it's both filling and, while it has a great taste of its own, the texture of the florets captures the sauce. In this recipe we used a hot vindaloo paste, but any Indian curry paste would work just as well.

cauliflower and green pea curry

You need 3 hard-boiled eggs for this recipe.

600g (1¼ pounds) cauliflower florets

2 tablespoons ghee

1 medium brown onion (150g), chopped finely

2 cloves garlic, crushed

1 teaspoon grated ginger

¼ cup (75g) hot curry paste

¾ cup (180ml) pouring cream

2 large tomatoes (440g), chopped coarsely

1 cup (120g) frozen peas

1 cup (280g) yoghurt

3 hard-boiled eggs, sliced thinly

¼ cup finely chopped fresh coriander (cilantro)

1 Microwave cauliflower until almost tender; drain.
2 Meanwhile, heat ghee in a large saucepan over medium-high heat; cook onion, garlic and ginger, stirring, for 5 minutes or until onion softens. Add paste; cook, stirring, until mixture is fragrant.
3 Add cream to pan; bring to the boil then reduce heat. Add cauliflower and tomato; simmer, uncovered, for 5 minutes, stirring occasionally.
4 Add peas and yoghurt; stir over low heat for 5 minutes or until peas are just cooked. Season to taste.
5 Serve curry sprinkled with egg and coriander.

prep + cook time 40 minutes serves 4
nutritional count per serving 40.9g total fat
(21.9g saturated fat); 2132kJ (510 cal);
15.5g carbohydrate; 17g protein; 8.6g fibre

chicken and pea pilaf

cooking-oil spray

625g (1¼ pounds) chicken thigh fillets, chopped coarsely

1½ cups (300g) white long-grain rice

1½ cups (375ml) chicken stock

¾ cup (180ml) water

1 cup (120g) frozen peas

½ cup coarsely chopped fresh flat-leaf parsley

¼ cup (35g) toasted slivered almonds

1 Spray a large saucepan with oil; cook chicken over high heat, in batches, until browned.

2 Return chicken to pan with rice, stock and the water; bring to the boil. Reduce heat; simmer, covered tightly, for 5 minutes.

3 Sprinkle peas over rice; simmer, covered tightly, for 10 minutes or until rice is tender and liquid is absorbed.

4 Remove from heat; stand, covered, for 5 minutes. Stir in parsley; season to taste. Serve pilaf sprinkled with nuts.

prep + cook time 25 minutes **serves** 4
nutritional count per serving 17g total fat
(4g saturated fat); 2362kJ (565 cal);
62.1g carbohydrate; 38.7g protein; 3.5g fibre

serving suggestion Steamed asparagus or broccolini.
tip The recipe is best made close to serving.

minted lamb vermicelli soup

100g (3½ ounces) bean thread vermicelli

1 tablespoon peanut oil

600g (1¼ pounds) lamb fillets, sliced thinly

2 tablespoons finely chopped fresh lemon grass

2 teaspoons bottled chopped chilli

4 teaspoons finely grated ginger

4 cloves garlic, crushed

⅓ cup (80ml) fish sauce

1.5 litres (6 cups) chicken stock

1 tablespoon white (granulated) sugar

500g (1 pound) asparagus, trimmed, chopped coarsely

¼ cup finely chopped fresh coriander (cilantro)

⅓ cup finely chopped fresh mint

8 green onions (scallions), chopped finely

4 medium tomatoes (760g), seeded, sliced thinly

1 Place vermicelli in a large heatproof bowl, cover with boiling water; stand until just tender, drain.

2 Meanwhile, heat half the oil in a large saucepan over high heat; cook lamb, in batches, until browned. Remove from pan.

3 Heat remaining oil in same pan over medium heat; cook lemon grass, chilli, ginger and garlic, stirring, for 1 minute or until fragrant. Add sauce, stock and sugar; cook, stirring, until mixture boils.

4 Add asparagus; simmer, uncovered, until asparagus is just tender. Add herbs, onion, tomato, vermicelli and lamb to pan; stir until soup is hot.

prep + cook time 30 minutes **serves** 6
nutritional count per serving 10g total fat
(3.2g saturated fat); 1041kJ (249 cal);
11.1g carbohydrate; 27.6g protein; 2.4g fibre

tip This recipe is best made close to serving.

saganaki prawns

1 tablespoon olive oil

1 medium white onion (150g), chopped finely

4 cloves garlic, crushed

410g (13 ounces) canned crushed tomatoes

¾ cup (180ml) dry white wine

2kg (4 pounds) uncooked medium king prawns (shrimp)

¼ cup coarsely chopped fresh flat-leaf parsley

¼ cup coarsely chopped fresh oregano

200g (6½-ounce) piece fetta, crumbled

1 Heat oil in a large frying pan over medium heat; cook onion and garlic, stirring, for 5 minutes or until onion softens. Add tomatoes and wine; bring to the boil. Reduce heat; simmer, covered, for 10 minutes, stirring occasionally.

2 Meanwhile, shell and devein prawns leaving tails intact. Add prawns and herbs to tomato mixture; simmer, covered, for 10 minutes, stirring occasionally.

3 Meanwhile, preheat grill (broiler).

4 Sprinkle fetta over prawn mixture; grill, uncovered, until fetta browns lightly.

prep + cook time 40 minutes **serves** 4
nutritional count per serving 18g total fat (8.6g saturated fat); 1956kJ (468 cal); 5.8g carbohydrate; 61.8g protein; 2.4g fibre

tips Saganaki, despite sounding vaguely Japanese, is the traditional Greek name for a snack or entrée of grilled or fried cheese (fetta, kasseri, haloumi or kefalograviera), which is then sprinkled with lemon juice and eaten with bread. It has evolved, however, into a descriptive culinary term for any dish that uses cooked cheese as one of the main ingredients, such as the saganaki prawns in this recipe.

tips You can use vegetable stock instead of the chicken consommé. Stir a little chopped preserved lemon and fresh tarragon into the rice, if you like.

asparagus and zucchini rice

¾ cup (180ml) chicken consommé

1 large zucchini (150g), chopped coarsely

185g (6 ounces) asparagus, trimmed, chopped coarsely

500g (1 pound) microwavable brown medium-grain rice

2 tablespoons finely chopped fresh flat-leaf parsley

1 cup (80g) finely grated parmesan

1 Combine consommé, zucchini and asparagus in a deep frying pan; bring to the boil, simmer, uncovered, until liquid is reduced by half.
2 Add rice and parsley; cook, stirring, until hot. Stir in parmesan; season to taste. Serve topped with extra parmesan, if you like.

prep + cook time 20 minutes **serves** 4
nutritional count per serving 5.4g total fat
(3g saturated fat); 840kJ (201 cal);
27.6g carbohydrate; 9.2g protein; 2.2g fibre

serving suggestion Tomato and rocket salad.

tip We used desiree potatoes, which are red-skinned, moist-fleshed, multi-purpose potatoes. You could use red eye, pontiac or baby new potatoes.

italian-style lamb cutlets

2 large potatoes (600g), unpeeled

2 tablespoons olive oil

1 fresh bay leaf

1 medium red onion (170g), cut into 8 wedges

12 french-trimmed lamb cutlets (600g)

285g (9 ounces) bottled roasted red capsicums (bell peppers) in oil, drained

⅓ cup (50g) drained sun-dried tomatoes in oil

½ cup (90g) pitted green olives

2 tablespoons fresh oregano leaves

¼ cup (60ml) beef stock

1 medium lemon (140g)

1 Wash unpeeled potatoes, then slice thinly. Heat oil in a large frying pan over medium-high heat; cook potato, with crushed bay leaf, turning, for 5 minutes or until potato is browned lightly.
2 Add onion to pan; cook, covered, stirring occasionally, for 5 minutes or until onion softens and potato is tender.
3 Move potato mixture to the centre of the pan. Season lamb, place around outside edge of pan; cook until lamb is browned both sides.
4 Add capsicum, tomatoes, half the olives, oregano and stock to pan; bring to the boil. Reduce heat; simmer, covered, for 3 minutes or until lamb is cooked as desired. Season to taste.
5 Meanwhile, finely grate lemon rind; juice lemon. Serve lamb mixture sprinkled with rind, drizzled with juice and topped with remaining olives.

prep + cook time 30 minutes serves 4
nutritional count per serving 18.9g total fat (5.1g saturated fat); 1747kJ (418 cal); 34.1g carbohydrate; 23.9g protein; 6.4g fibre

serving suggestion Green leafy salad.

stir-fries

A tasty stir-fry is an easy way to get kids to eat their vegetables. Add a variety of asian vegetables for an authentic stir-fry flavour.

pork larb with rice noodles

200g (6½ ounces) fresh rice stick noodles

1 tablespoon peanut oil

600g (1¼ pounds) minced (ground) pork

10cm (2-inch) stick lemon grass (20g), chopped finely

1 clove garlic, crushed

2 teaspoons sambal oelek

2 tablespoons lime juice

2 tablespoons brown sugar

1 tablespoon fish sauce

3 green onions (scallions), sliced thinly

1 fresh long red chilli, sliced thinly

¼ cup loosely packed fresh coriander leaves (cilantro)

lime cheeks or wedges, to serve

1 Cook rice noodles in a medium saucepan of boiling water for 2 minutes or until tender; drain.

2 Meanwhile, heat oil in a large frying pan over high heat; stir-fry pork until browned. Add lemon grass, garlic and sambal oelek; stir-fry for 1 minute or until fragrant. Add juice, sugar and sauce; stir-fry for 1 minute. Remove from heat; stir in onion. Season to taste.

3 Serve pork mixture on rice noodles; sprinkle with chilli and coriander, accompany with lime cheeks.

prep + cook time 20 minutes **serves** 4
nutritional count per serving 18.9g total fat
(6g saturated fat); 1546kJ (369 cal);
16.6g carbohydrate; 32.9g protein; 0.9g fibre

serving suggestion Steamed asian greens.

tip You can slice the beef yourself if you prefer. Use fillet, scotch fillet or rump for best results.

ginger teriyaki beef

⅓ cup (80ml) teriyaki sauce

½ cup (125ml) hoisin sauce

2 tablespoons mirin

1 tablespoon peanut oil

750g (1½ pounds) beef strips

250g (8 ounces) broccoli, cut into florets

250g (8 ounces) sugar snap peas, trimmed

115g (3½ ounces) fresh baby corn, halved lengthways

1 teaspoon finely grated ginger

1½ cups (120g) bean sprouts

1 Combine sauces and mirin in a small jug.

2 Heat half the oil in a wok over high heat; stir-fry beef, in batches, until browned. Remove from wok.

3 Heat the remaining oil in wok; stir-fry broccoli until almost tender.

4 Return beef to wok with sauce mixture, peas, corn and ginger. Stir-fry until vegetables and beef are cooked. Remove from heat; sprinkle with sprouts.

prep + cook time 20 minutes **serves** 4
nutritional count per serving 20.7g total fat
(7.2g saturated fat); 2073kJ (496 cal);
23.2g carbohydrate; 48g protein; 10.5g fibre

serving suggestion Steamed white rice or thick rice noodles.

tips Thai basil, also known as horapa, has a slight licorice or aniseed taste. Use sweet basil if thai basil is unavailable. Thai chilli jam is a combination of garlic, shallots, chilli, tomato paste, fish sauce, galangal, spices and shrimp paste. It is sold under various names, and can be found in the Asian food section of most supermarkets.

chilli jam beef noodles

250g (8 ounces) dried rice stick noodles

625g (1¼ pounds) beef eye fillet, sliced thinly

2 tablespoons thai chilli jam

1 medium red capsicum (bell pepper) (200g), sliced thinly

155g (5 ounces) sugar snap peas, trimmed

¼ cup (60ml) water

½ cup loosely packed fresh thai basil leaves

1 Place noodles in a large heatproof bowl, cover with boiling water; stand until tender, drain.

2 Meanwhile, combine beef and half the chilli jam in a medium bowl. Stir-fry beef, in batches, in an oiled wok over high heat until browned; remove from wok.

3 Add capsicum to wok; stir-fry for 1 minute or until tender. Return beef to wok with noodles, peas, the water and remaining chilli jam; stir-fry until hot. Season to taste; serve sprinkled with thai basil.

prep + cook time 25 minutes serves 4
nutritional count per serving 9.9g total fat
(4g saturated fat); 1195kJ (286 cal);
12.2g carbohydrate; 35.6g protein; 2.1g fibre

honey ginger chicken

500g (1 pound) chicken thigh fillets, chopped coarsely

1 teaspoon finely grated ginger

1 teaspoon chinese five-spice powder

2 tablespoons peanut oil

170g (5½ ounces) asparagus, trimmed, cut into 3cm (1¼-inch) lengths

2 tablespoons dark soy sauce

2 tablespoons honey

1 tablespoon water

250g (8 ounces) snow peas, trimmed, halved

1 Combine chicken, ginger, five-spice and half the oil in a medium bowl.
2 Heat half the remaining oil in a wok over high heat; stir-fry chicken, in batches, until browned. Remove from wok.
3 Heat remaining oil in wok; stir-fry asparagus until tender. Return chicken to wok with sauce, honey, the water and peas; stir-fry until hot. Season to taste.

prep + cook time 25 minutes **serves** 4
nutritional count per serving 15.5g total fat (3.5g saturated fat); 1292kJ (309 cal); 15.6g carbohydrate; 26.4g protein; 2.1g fibre

serving suggestion Steamed jasmine rice.
tip Chicken mixture can be marinated overnight for a more intense flavour.

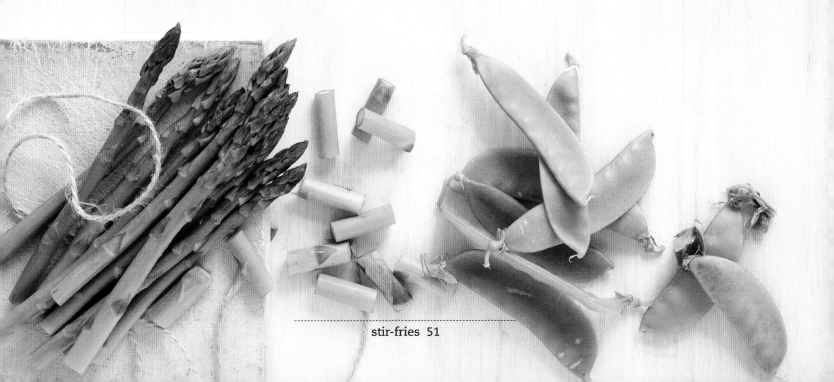

char siu pork, corn and choy sum

2 tablespoons peanut oil

600g (1¼ pounds) pork fillets, sliced thinly

2 medium brown onions (300g), cut into thin wedges

230g (7 ounces) baby corn

300g (9½ ounces) choy sum, trimmed, chopped coarsely

2 tablespoons char siu sauce

2 teaspoons light soy sauce

2 teaspoons lime juice

1 fresh long red chilli, sliced thinly

1 Heat half the oil in a wok over high heat; stir-fry pork, in batches, until browned and cooked through.
2 Heat remaining oil in wok; stir-fry onion and corn until onion softens and corn is tender.
3 Return pork to wok with choy sum, sauces and juice; stir-fry until hot. Sprinkle with chilli.

prep + cook time 25 minutes **serves** 4
nutritional count per serving 14g total fat
(3g saturated fat); 1513kJ (362 cal);
18.4g carbohydrate; 37.5g protein; 5.7g fibre

serving suggestion Steamed white rice or noodles.

wok-tossed honey and soy chicken wings

12 large chicken wings (1.5kg)

2 teaspoons crushed garlic

1 tablespoon finely grated ginger

1 tablespoon peanut oil

1 tablespoon fish sauce

1 tablespoon soy sauce

¼ cup (90g) honey

2 green onions (scallions), sliced thinly

1 Cut and discard wing tips from chicken; cut wings in half at joint. Combine chicken, garlic and ginger in a large bowl.

2 Heat oil in a wok over high heat; stir-fry chicken mixture, in batches, until chicken is browned.

3 Return chicken mixture to wok. Add sauces and honey; stir-fry until well coated. Cover wok; cook, stirring occasionally, for 10 minutes or until chicken is cooked through. Serve topped with onion.

prep + cook time 30 minutes **serves** 4
nutritional count per serving 43.1g total fat
(11.5g saturated fat); 2905kJ (695 cal);
19.1g carbohydrate; 59g protein; 0.4g fibre

ASIAN VEGIES

sweet and sour vegetables

Heat 1 tablespoon peanut oil in a wok; stir-fry 800g (1½lb) packaged traditional stir-fry vegetables and 115g (3½oz) coarsely chopped baby corn until vegetables are tender. Add 225g (7oz) canned drained pineapple pieces, ½ cup sweet and sour sauce and 50g (1½oz) enoki mushrooms; stir-fry until hot, season to taste.

prep + cook time 15 minutes **serves** 4
nutritional count per serving 5.4g total fat (0.9g saturated fat); 890kJ (213 cal); 31.8g carbohydrate; 5.2g protein; 8.8g fibre

grilled asian vegetables

Boil, steam or microwave 400g (12oz) trimmed, halved baby pak choy until wilted; drain. Brush with 1 tablespoon peanut oil; cook on a heated oiled barbecue flat plate until tender. Cut 200g (6oz) baby corn in half lengthways; combine in a large bowl with 175g (5oz) halved broccolini, 100g (3oz) trimmed snow peas and an extra 1 tablespoon peanut oil; mix well. Cook vegetables on flat plate until tender. Meanwhile, combine 2 tablespoons mirin, 1 tablespoon each of oyster sauce and light soy sauce, 1 crushed garlic clove, 1 teaspoon white (granulated) sugar and ½ teaspoon sesame oil in same bowl; mix in vegetables.

prep + cook time 25 minutes **serves** 4
nutritional count per serving 11.2g total fat (1.9g saturated fat); 948kJ (226 cal); 16.7g carbohydrate; 8.7g protein; 8.6g fibre

steamed asian greens with char siu sauce

Layer 350g (11oz) trimmed broccolini, 150g (4½oz) trimmed snow peas, 2 halved baby buk choy and 1 thinly sliced fresh long red chilli in a large baking-paper-lined bamboo steamer. Steam, covered, over a large wok of simmering water about 5 minutes or until vegetables are just tender. Combine vegetables, 2 tablespoons char siu sauce and 2 teaspoons sesame oil in a large bowl. Heat 1 tablespoon peanut oil in a small saucepan until hot; pour oil over vegetable mixture then toss to combine. Serve sprinkled with 1 tablespoon toasted sesame seeds.

prep + cook time 25 minutes **serves** 4
nutritional count per serving 9.5g total fat (1.4g saturated fat); 635kJ (152 cal); 7g carbohydrate; 6.6g protein; 6.6g fibre

hot, sweet and sour mixed vegetables

Heat 1 tablespoon oil in a wok; stir-fry 15g (½oz) grated ginger, 2 crushed garlic cloves and 2 finely chopped fresh red thai (serrano) chillies until fragrant. Thinly slice 1 red and yellow capsicum; cut 230g (7oz) fresh baby corn in half. Add to wok; stir-fry until tender. Add ¼ cup vegetable stock and 2 tablespoons each of grated palm sugar, tamarind concentrate and oyster sauce; stir-fry for 2 minutes. Coarsely chop 150g (4½oz) oyster mushrooms, 350g (11oz) baby buk choy and 280g (9oz) gai lan; add to wok; stir-fry until greens wilt. Remove from heat; stir in 6 green onions (scallions), cut into 3cm (1¼ inch) lengths and ½ cup firmly packed vietnamese mint leaves.

prep + cook time 30 minutes **serves** 4
nutritional count per serving 6.1g total fat (1g saturated fat); 861kJ (206 cal); 25.8g carbohydrate; 7.9g protein; 8.5g fibre

sang choy bow

2 teaspoons sesame oil

1 small brown onion (80g), chopped finely

2 cloves garlic, crushed

1 teaspoon finely grated fresh ginger

500g (1 pound) minced (ground) pork

2 tablespoons water

100g (3 ounces) shiitake mushrooms, chopped finely

2 tablespoons light soy sauce

2 tablespoons oyster sauce

1 tablespoon lime juice

2 cups (160g) bean sprouts

4 green onions (scallions), sliced thinly

¼ cup coarsely chopped fresh coriander (cilantro)

12 large butter (boston) lettuce leaves

1 Heat oil in a wok over high heat; stir-fry brown onion, garlic and ginger until onion softens. Add pork; stir-fry until changed in colour.

2 Add the water, mushrooms, sauces and juice; stir-fry until mushrooms are tender. Remove from heat.

3 Add sprouts, green onion and coriander; toss to combine.

4 Spoon sang choy bow into lettuce leaves to serve.

prep + cook time 30 minutes **serves** 4
nutritional count per serving 11.5g total fat
(3.6g saturated fat); 1112kJ (266 cal);
8.9g carbohydrate; 29.3g protein; 4.1g fibre

tip Pork mixture can be made a day ahead to the end of step 2. Reheat, then continue from step 3.

spiced tofu with lemon chilli sauce

½ cup (125ml) sweet chilli sauce

2 teaspoons finely grated lemon rind

¼ cup (60ml) lemon juice

440g (14-ounce) packet fresh egg noodles

⅓ cup (50g) plain (all-purpose) flour

2 teaspoons chinese five-spice powder

300g (9½ ounces) firm tofu, cut into 2cm (¾-inch) pieces

1 tablespoon olive oil

1 large brown onion (200g), chopped coarsely

3 cloves garlic, sliced thinly

1 small yellow capsicum (bell pepper) (150g), sliced thinly

300g (9½ ounces) sugar snap peas, trimmed

1 Combine sauce, rind and juice in a small saucepan; bring to the boil. Remove from heat.

2 Place noodles in a large heatproof bowl; cover with boiling water; separate with a fork, drain.

3 Combine flour and five-spice in a medium bowl, add tofu; toss to coat tofu in flour mixture. Shake away excess flour.

4 Heat half the oil in a wok over high heat; stir-fry tofu, in batches, until browned all over. Remove from wok.

5 Heat remaining oil in wok; stir-fry onion, garlic and capsicum until onion softens. Add noodles, peas and half the lemon chilli sauce; stir-fry until peas are just tender. Add tofu to noodle mixture; toss to combine.

6 Drizzle noodles with remaining lemon chilli sauce to serve.

prep + cook time 40 minutes **serves** 4
nutritional count per serving 12.2g total fat
(1.8g saturated fat); 2241kJ (536 cal);
80.3g carbohydrate; 24.6g protein; 8.5g fibre

prawn and noodle stir-fry

500g (1 pound) uncooked medium king prawns (shrimp)

200g (6½ ounces) dried rice stick noodles

1 clove garlic, crushed

2 tablespoons japanese soy sauce

2 tablespoons fish sauce

1 teaspoon sambal oelek

1 cup (80g) bean sprouts

¼ cup loosely packed fresh coriander leaves (cilantro)

1 Shell and devein prawns leaving tails intact.
2 Place noodles in a large heatproof bowl, cover with boiling water; stand until just tender, drain.
3 Meanwhile, heat oiled wok over high heat; stir-fry prawns and garlic until prawns are just changed in colour. Add noodles, sauces and sambal; gently stir-fry until hot. Stir in bean sprouts and coriander.

prep + cook time 30 minutes **serves** 4
nutritional count per serving 1.1g total fat
(0.1g saturated fat); 506kJ (121 cal);
11g carbohydrate; 15.7g protein; 1.2g fibre

tip You can use beef strips instead of the mince, if you prefer.

beef in black bean sauce with rice noodles

250g (8 ounces) dried rice stick noodles

1 tablespoon peanut oil

600g (1¼ pounds) minced (ground) beef

1 medium brown onion (150g), sliced thinly

2 fresh long red chillies, sliced thinly

350g (11 ounces) wombok (napa cabbage), chopped coarsely

150g (4½ ounces) sugar snap peas

¼ cup (60ml) black bean sauce

¼ cup (60ml) kecap manis

¼ cup (60ml) beef stock

1 tablespoon rice vinegar

4 green onions (scallions), sliced thinly

1 Place noodles in a large heatproof bowl, cover with boiling water; stand until just tender, drain.

2 Meanwhile, heat oil in a wok over high heat; stir-fry beef, brown onion and chillies until beef is cooked through. Add wombok and peas; stir-fry until wombok is tender. Add noodles, sauces, stock, vinegar and green onions; stir-fry until hot.

prep + cook time 30 minutes **serves** 4
nutritional count per serving 16.4g total fat
(6.4g saturated fat); 1559kJ (373 cal);
19.2g carbohydrate; 35.2g protein; 3.3g fibre

garlic seafood stir-fry

1kg (2 pounds) uncooked medium king prawns (shrimp)

500g (1 pound) cleaned baby squid hoods

¼ cup (60ml) peanut oil

1 tablespoon finely chopped coriander (cilantro) root and stem mixture

2 fresh small red thai (serrano) chillies

½ teaspoon coarsely ground black pepper

4 cloves garlic, crushed

170g (5½ ounces) asparagus, trimmed, chopped coarsely

175g (5½ ounces) broccolini, chopped coarsely

1 cup (80g) bean sprouts

2 green onions (scallions), sliced thinly

2 tablespoons coarsely chopped fresh coriander (cilantro)

lime wedges, to serve

1 Shell and devein prawns leaving tails intact.

2 Cut squid down centre to open out; score inside in a diagonal pattern then cut into thick strips.

3 Heat half the oil in a wok; stir-fry seafood, in batches, until prawns change in colour. Remove from wok.

4 Heat remaining oil in wok; stir-fry coriander mixture, chilli, pepper and garlic until fragrant. Add asparagus and broccolini; stir-fry until vegetables are almost tender. Return seafood to wok with sprouts; stir-fry until hot.

5 Serve stir-fry sprinkled with onion and chopped coriander; accompany with lime wedges.

prep + cook time 40 minutes   **serves** 4
nutritional count per serving 16.2g total fat
(3.1g saturated fat); 1509kJ (361 cal);
1.6g carbohydrate; 50.3g protein; 3.7g fibre

serving suggestion Steamed jasmine rice.
tips When you buy a bunch of coriander (cilantro) at your local greengrocer, it is one of the very few fresh herbs that come with its stems and roots intact. Wash the leaves, stems and roots well before chopping them, and also scrape the roots with a small flat knife to remove some of the outer fibrous skin. After removing the leaves, finely or coarsely chop the roots and stems to use in curry pastes or recipes like this stir-fry.

chicken, vegetable and almond stir-fry

2½ cups (500g) jasmine rice

2 tablespoons peanut oil

625g (1¼ pounds) chicken breast fillets, sliced thinly

1 medium brown onion (150g), sliced thinly

2 cloves garlic, crushed

345g (11 ounces) broccolini, trimmed, chopped coarsely

125g (4 ounces) fresh baby corn, halved lengthways

155g (5 ounces) sugar snap peas, trimmed

⅓ cup (45g) toasted slivered almonds

1 tablespoon fish sauce

1 tablespoon sweet chilli sauce

⅓ cup thai basil leaves

1 Cook rice in a large saucepan of boiling water until just tender; drain. Cover to keep warm.

2 Meanwhile, heat half the oil in a wok over high heat; stir-fry chicken, in batches, until browned lightly and cooked through. Remove from wok.

3 Heat remaining oil in wok; stir-fry onion and garlic until onion softens. Add broccolini, corn and peas; stir-fry until vegetables are tender.

4 Return chicken to wok with nuts and sauces; stir-fry until heated through. Sprinkle stir-fry with basil; serve with rice.

prep + cook time 30 minutes **serves** 4
nutritional count per serving 20.2g total fat
(3.1g saturated fat); 3515kJ (841 cal);
109.4g carbohydrate; 50.5g protein; 7.5g fibre

tips You can use vegetables of your choice; broccoli, asian greens, asparagus and capsicum (bell pepper) would all work well. Use packet microwave rice for a faster option.

stir-fried lamb in hoisin sauce

2 tablespoons peanut oil

600g (1¼ pounds) lamb strips

2 cloves garlic, crushed

1 teaspoon finely grated ginger

1 medium brown onion (150g), sliced thinly

1 small red capsicum (bell pepper) (150g), sliced thinly

1 small yellow capsicum (bell pepper) (150g), sliced thinly

6 green onions (scallions), sliced thinly

⅓ cup (80ml) chicken stock

1 tablespoon soy sauce

¼ cup (60ml) hoisin sauce

1 Heat half the oil in a wok over high heat; stir-fry lamb, in batches, until browned all over. Remove from wok.
2 Heat remaining oil in same wok; stir-fry garlic, ginger and brown onion until onion is just tender. Add capsicum and green onion; stir-fry until capsicum is just tender.
3 Return lamb to wok with combined stock and sauces; stir-fry until sauce boils and thickens slightly.

prep + cook time 30 minutes **serves** 4
nutritional count per serving 24.5g total fat
(7.8g saturated fat); 1672kJ (400 cal);
11.6g carbohydrate; 34.1g protein; 3.5g fibre

serving suggestion Steamed rice or noodles accompanied with steamed asian greens.

tip Fried garlic (may be labelled as 'kratiem jiew') is an Asian condiment usually served sprinkled on top of just-cooked dishes. It is found at Asian grocery stores; once opened, it will keep for months if tightly sealed.

pork and gai lan stir-fry

500g (1 pound) fresh singapore noodles

2 tablespoons peanut oil

750g (1½ pounds) pork strips

1 large brown onion (200g), sliced into thick wedges

1 teaspoon crushed garlic

1kg (2 pounds) gai lan, chopped coarsely, leaves and stems separated

⅓ cup (80ml) oyster sauce

1 tablespoon soy sauce

1 Place noodles in a large heatproof bowl, cover with boiling water; stir gently to separate noodles, drain.

2 Heat half the oil in a wok over high heat; stir-fry pork, in batches, until browned and cooked through.

3 Heat remaining oil in wok; stir-fry onion and garlic until onion is soft. Add gai lan stems, stir-fry for 1 minute. Return pork to wok with gai lan leaves, combined sauces and noodles; stir-fry until gai lan is just wilted. Served sprinkled with fried garlic, if you like (see tip).

prep + cook time 15 minutes **serves** 4
nutritional count per serving 18.3g total fat (4.8g saturated fat); 3093kJ (740 cal); 75.4g carbohydrate; 60.3g protein; 12.4g fibre

grills & barbecues

These recipes work well all year – cook outside on the barbecue during summer and use your grill inside in the colder months.

fillet steak with creamy mustard sauce

8 baby new potatoes (chats) (320g), halved

200g (6½ ounces) baby green beans, trimmed

4 beef fillet steaks (500g)

2 tablespoons olive oil

⅓ cup loosely packed fresh basil leaves

creamy mustard sauce

30g (1 ounce) butter

2 teaspoons bottled crushed garlic

¼ cup (60ml) dry white wine

300ml thickened (heavy) cream

2 teaspoons dijon mustard

1 Boil, steam or microwave potato and beans, separately, until just tender.

2 Make creamy mustard sauce.

3 Heat an oiled grill pan (or grill plate or barbecue). Rub beef with oil, season; cook beef for 3 minutes each side or until cooked as desired. Remove from heat; cover to keep warm.

4 Serve beef with potato and beans; drizzle with creamy mustard sauce and sprinkle with basil.

creamy mustard sauce Melt butter in a medium saucepan; cook garlic, stirring, until fragrant. Add wine; bring to the boil. Reduce heat; simmer, uncovered, until liquid is reduced by half. Add cream and mustard; simmer, uncovered, stirring occasionally, until sauce thickens. Season to taste.

prep + cook time 20 minutes (+ standing) **serves** 4
nutritional count per serving 52.2g total fat
(27.3g saturated fat); 2804kJ (670 cal);
14.6g carbohydrate; 32.5g protein; 3.4g fibre

tips Quarter the potatoes if they are large. You can use wholegrain mustard in place of the dijon mustard if preferred. For a lower-fat version, use light cream. Scotch fillet, sirloin and rump steak are also suitable for this recipe; thinner steaks will take less cooking time.

tips Dijonnaise is a blend of mayonnaise and dijon mustard; plain mayonnaise or aïoli can be used instead, or spread sandwiches with your favourite chutney, relish or sauce. Try sourdough bread instead of the ciabatta.

steak sandwiches

4 beef scotch fillet steaks (600g)

¼ cup (75g) dijonnaise

8 thick slices ciabatta bread (400g), toasted

50g (1½ ounces) mixed salad leaves

2 medium tomatoes (300g), sliced thickly

⅓ cup (110g) capsicum relish

1 Season steaks well on both sides. Cook steaks on a heated oiled barbecue (or grill or grill pan) over high heat until browned on both sides and cooked as desired. Remove from heat; cover to keep warm.

2 Spread dijonnaise on toasted bread slices. Sandwich salad leaves, steaks, tomato and relish between toast slices.

prep + cook time 10 minutes **serves** 4
nutritional count per serving 15.9g total fat
(4.7g saturated fat); 2646kJ (633 cal);
72.1g carbohydrate; 45.4g protein; 8.4g fibre

za'atar lamb chops
with roasted garlic yoghurt

8 cloves garlic

1 teaspoon olive oil

1 cup (280g) greek-style yoghurt

8 lamb loin chops (800g)

⅓ cup loosely packed fresh flat-leaf parsley leaves

lemon cheeks or wedges, to serve

za'atar

1 tablespoon sesame seeds

1 tablespoon sumac

1 tablespoon finely chopped fresh thyme

1 tablespoon olive oil

1 Preheat oven to 180°C/350°F.

2 Place unpeeled garlic on a baking tray; drizzle with oil. Roast for 10 minutes. When cool enough to handle, peel garlic and place in a small bowl; mash with a fork. Add yoghurt; stir to combine.

3 Meanwhile, cook lamb on a heated oiled grill plate (or grill or barbecue) for 4 minutes each side or until cooked as desired. Remove from heat; cover to keep warm.

4 Meanwhile, make za'atar.

5 Add za'atar to lamb; toss to coat. Season to taste.

6 Sprinkle lamb with parsley; accompany with garlic yoghurt, and lemon cheeks.

za'atar Dry-fry sesame seeds in a small frying pan, shaking pan until seeds are golden. Add sumac; shake pan until fragrant. Transfer to a small bowl; stir in thyme and oil.

prep + cook time 30 minutes **serves** 4
nutritional count per serving 40.2g total fat
(15.5g saturated fat); 2311kJ (552 cal);
0.7g carbohydrate; 36.3g protein; 2.2g fibre

serving suggestion Tomato and herb salad.

grilled prawns with lemon grass and lime

60g (2 ounces) butter, softened

10cm (4-inch) stick lemon grass (20g), chopped finely

2 teaspoons finely grated lime rind

2 tablespoons lime juice

2 tablespoons finely chopped fresh flat-leaf parsley

500g (1 pound) shelled uncooked medium king prawns (shrimp)

lime cheeks or wedges, to serve

1 Beat butter, lemon grass, rind and juice in a small bowl until combined; stir in parsley.

2 Melt half the butter mixture in a large frying pan; remove from heat, stir in prawns.

3 Cook prawns on a heated oiled barbecue (or grill or grill pan) over high heat until changed in colour. Serve prawns topped with remaining butter mixture and lime cheeks.

prep + cook time 10 minutes **serves** 4
nutritional count per serving 13.1g total fat
(8.2g saturated fat); 928kJ (222 cal);
0.3g carbohydrate; 25.9g protein; 0.2g fibre

serving suggestion Green salad and crusty bread.
tips Use the white part only of the lemon grass. If you buy the prawns whole and shell them yourself, you will need 1kg (2 pounds).

miso fish with daikon salad

2 tablespoons white miso paste

¼ cup (60ml) mirin

4 snapper fillets (800g)

3 lebanese cucumbers (390g), sliced into thin ribbons

1 daikon radish (450g), sliced thinly

4 red radishes (140g), sliced thinly

⅓ cup (80ml) rice wine vinegar

1 tablespoon mirin, extra

1 teaspoon japanese soy sauce

270g (8½ ounces) soba noodles

1 tablespoon white sesame seeds

½ teaspoon black sesame seeds

2 green onions (scallions), sliced thinly lengthways

1 Preheat grill (broiler). Bring a large saucepan of water to the boil.

2 Combine miso and mirin in a small bowl. Place fish on an oiled oven tray; spoon miso mixture over fish. Grill fish for 3 minutes each side, basting with miso mixture, or until just cooked through.

3 Combine cucumber, daikon and radish with vinegar, extra mirin and sauce in a large bowl; season to taste.

4 Cook noodles in the boiling water until just tender, drain; rinse under cold water, drain.

5 Sprinkle fish with sesame seeds; serve with daikon salad and noodles, top with onion.

prep + cook time 20 minutes **serves** 4
nutritional count per serving 10g total fat
(3.5g saturated fat); 1678kJ (401 cal);
22.2g carbohydrate; 46.6g protein; 6.1g fibre

tips For faster slicing, use a mandoline or V-slicer to slice the cucumbers, daikon and radishes. Both black and white sesame seeds are used in Japanese cooking; white sesame seeds have a nutty flavour, while black sesame seeds taste more bitter.

caprese chicken

2 chicken breast fillets (500g)

1 teaspoon bottled crushed garlic

1 tablespoon olive oil

1 large tomato (220g), sliced thinly

100g (3 ounces) mozzarella, sliced thinly

½ cup loosely packed fresh basil leaves

2 x 475g (15-ounce) tubs mashed potato

2 tablespoons rinsed, drained capers

¼ cup (60ml) olive oil, extra

1 tablespoon, rinsed, drained capers, extra

1 bunch rocket (100g)

1 Preheat grill (broiler).

2 Slice chicken in half horizontally. Combine chicken, garlic and oil in a medium bowl; season.

3 Transfer chicken to an oven tray; grill chicken for 3 minutes each side or until browned.

4 Top chicken with tomato, cheese and basil. Grill 3 minutes or until tomato is softened slightly and chicken is cooked.

5 Meanwhile, microwave mashed potato according to directions on tub. Stir capers through potato; season to taste.

6 Heat extra oil in a small frying pan over medium-high heat; cook extra capers, stirring, for 1 minute. Remove capers with a slotted spoon; drain on kitchen paper.

7 Serve chicken with mashed potato and rocket; sprinkle over extra capers.

prep + cook time 20 minutes **serves** 4
nutritional count per serving 4.7g total fat
(5.5g saturated fat); 1847kJ (441 cal);
32g carbohydrate; 41.5g protein; 4.7g fibre

tip Balsamic glaze is a thick reduction of balsamic vinegar; it is made from grape must (the freshly pressed grape juice from young grapes that contains the skins, seeds and stems of the fruit) and balsamic vinegar. It is available from most major supermarkets in the condiment/vinegar aisle.

mediterranean grilled lamb chops with black olive mash

1kg (2 pounds) potatoes, chopped coarsely

400g (13 ounces) mixed baby tomatoes, halved

1 cup loosely packed fresh baby basil leaves

¼ cup (60ml) balsamic glaze

⅓ cup (80ml) olive oil

8 lamb loin chops (800g)

½ cup (125ml) milk

1 clove garlic, crushed

1 cup (150g) sliced kalamata olives, drained

1 Place potato in a medium saucepan, cover with cold water, bring to the boil; boil for 10 minutes or until tender. Drain; cover to keep warm.

2 Meanwhile, combine tomato, basil, half the glaze and half the oil in a medium bowl; toss to combine.

3 Cook lamb on a heated oiled grill plate (or grill or barbecue) for 4 minutes each side or until cooked as desired. Cover to keep warm.

4 Heat milk in a small saucepan until hot (do not boil). Add milk, remaining oil and garlic to potato; mash until smooth. Stir in olives. Season to taste.

5 Serve lamb with tomato salad and black olive mash, drizzle with remaining balsamic glaze.

prep + cook time 35 minutes **serves** 4
nutritional count per serving 54.6g total fat
(16.4g saturated fat); 3476kJ (830 cal);
40.3g carbohydrate; 39.8g protein; 4.6g fibre

SKEWERS

hoisin pork skewers

Slice 750g (1½lb) pork fillet into thin strips; thread pork onto 12 skewers. Combine ½ cup hoisin sauce, 2 tablespoons plum sauce and 2 crushed garlic cloves in a small bowl. Cook skewers on a heated oiled barbecue, brushing frequently with sauce mixture, until browned and cooked through.

prep + cook time 20 minutes **makes** 12
nutritional count per skewer 6.3g total fat (1.8g saturated fat); 1313kJ (314 cal); 20g carbohydrate; 41.8g protein; 3.8g fibre

satay beef skewers

Combine ⅔ cup canned coconut cream, ¼ cup crunchy peanut butter, 1 crushed garlic clove, 1 finely chopped fresh small red thai (serrano) chilli, 1 tablespoon fish sauce and 1 tablespoon kecap manis in a medium jug. Cut 800g (1½lb) piece beef eye fillet into 3cm cubes; thread beef onto 8 bamboo skewers. Brush ½ cup of the satay sauce over beef. Cook skewers on heated oiled barbecue until cooked as desired. Bring remaining satay sauce to the boil in a small saucepan; drizzle over skewers.

prep + cook time 30 minutes **makes** 8
nutritional count per skewer 14.6g total fat (6.9g saturated fat); 993kJ (237 cal); 1.8g carbohydrate; 24.2g protein; 1.4g fibre

salt and pepper chicken skewers

Coarsely chop 8 chicken thigh fillets; thread chicken onto 12 skewers. Combine ½ teaspoon chinese five-spice, 1 teaspoon crushed sichuan peppercorns and 2 teaspoons sea salt in a small bowl; sprinkle mixture over chicken, then press on firmly. Cook chicken on a heated oiled barbecue until browned and cooked through.

prep + cook time 35 minutes **makes** 12
nutritional count per serving 14.5g total fat (4.4g saturated fat); 759kJ (181 cal); 0.4g carbohydrate; 12.4g protein; 0g fibre

spicy fish skewers

Cut 1kg (2lb) firm white fish fillets into 2cm cubes. Combine fish with 1 tablespoon each finely chopped fresh mint, coriander and fresh flat-leaf parsley, 2 finely chopped fresh small red thai (serrano) chillies, 2 tablespoons lemon juice and 1 tablespoon peanut oil in a medium bowl. Cut 4 x 10cm (4in) fresh lemon grass sticks in half lengthways; thread fish onto lemon grass skewers. Cook fish on a heated oiled barbecue until cooked through. Serve with lime wedges.

prep + cook time 25 minutes **makes** 8
nutritional count per serving 3.2g total fat (0.6g saturated fat); 493kJ (118 cal); 0.2g carbohydrate; 22g protein; 0.1g fibre

tips To save time, buy prawns already shelled from the fishmonger; you will need about 600g (1¼ pounds). Dukkah is found in the spice aisle of supermarkets. Cover the ends of the bamboo skewers in foil to prevent them from burning during cooking.

dukkah prawn skewers

1.2kg (2½ pounds) large uncooked king prawns (shrimp)

¼ cup (35g) pistachio dukkah

2 tablespoons olive oil

2 cloves garlic, crushed

2 teaspoons finely grated lemon rind

lemon wedges, to serve

1 Shell and devein prawns leaving tails intact.
2 Combine dukkah, oil, garlic and rind in a large bowl; add prawns, toss to coat in mixture.
3 Thread prawns onto 8 bamboo skewers. Cook skewers on a heated oiled grill plate (or grill or barbecue) until prawns change colour.
4 Accompany prawns with lemon wedges to serve.

prep + cook time 15 minutes serves 4
nutritional count per serving 14.5g total fat
(2g saturated fat); 1124kJ (269 cal);
1.5g carbohydrate; 32.6g protein; 1.1g fibre

serving suggestion Mixed salad leaves and steamed rice.

lamb cutlets in barbecue sauce

12 french-trimmed lamb cutlets (880g)

½ cup (125ml) barbecue sauce

1 tablespoon finely chopped fresh rosemary

2 cloves garlic, crushed

2 tablespoons olive oil

400g (13 ounces) green beans, trimmed

1 Place cutlets in a shallow dish; pour over combined sauce, rosemary, garlic and oil; season.
2 Cook cutlets on a heated oiled grill plate (or grill or barbecue) until cooked as you like.
3 Meanwhile, boil, steam or microwave beans until tender; drain. Serve cutlets with beans; season.

prep + cook time 15 minutes **serves** 4
nutritional count per serving 28.2g total fat
(9.9g saturated fat); 1793kJ (429 cal);
18.2g carbohydrate; 24.7g protein; 3.3g fibre

serving suggestion Mashed potato and steamed corn cobs.

tips You can use lamb loin chops if you prefer. Asparagus, broccoli or broccolini can be used in place of the beans.

satay pork medallions

4 pork loin steaks (600g)

¼ cup (70g) crunchy peanut butter

⅓ cup (80ml) coconut cream

2 tablespoons sweet chilli sauce

2 teaspoons fish sauce

¼ cup (60ml) water

1 tablespoon coarsely chopped fresh coriander (cilantro)

1 Cook steaks on a heated oiled grill plate (or grill or barbecue) over medium-high heat until browned on both sides and just cooked through.

2 Meanwhile, combine peanut butter, coconut cream, sauces and the water in a small saucepan; cook, stirring, over medium heat for 3 minutes or until thickened slightly.

3 Serve steaks drizzled with sauce; sprinkle with coriander.

prep + cook time 15 minutes **serves** 4
nutritional count per serving 23.9g total fat
(8.7g saturated fat); 1655kJ (396 cal);
4.6g carbohydrate; 39.7g protein; 2.8g fibre

serving suggestion Jasmine rice and steamed asian greens.
tip The satay sauce can be made up to 3 days ahead; reheat before serving.

lemon pepper pork with broad bean salad

4 pork cutlets (940g)

2 tablespoons lemon pepper seasoning

2 cups (360g) frozen broad (fava) beans

2 teaspoons finely grated lemon rind

2 tablespoons lemon juice

100g (3½ ounces) fetta, crumbled

¾ cup loosely packed fresh mint leaves, torn

1 Sprinkle cutlets on both sides with seasoning; cook on a heated oiled grill plate (or grill or barbecue) until browned on both sides and just cooked through.
2 Meanwhile, boil, steam or microwave beans until just tender; drain. When cool enough to handle, peel beans.
3 Combine beans, rind, juice, fetta and mint in a large bowl. Season to taste. Serve cutlets with salad.

prep + cook time 25 minutes **serves** 4
nutritional count per serving 24.1g total fat
(10g saturated fat); 1685kJ (403 cal);
2.6g carbohydrate; 41.2g protein; 6.3g fibre

serving suggestion Tomato and watercress salad.

tip This salad would also be delicious using baby peas instead of the broad beans.

barbecued salmon with minted peas and beans

4 x 155g (5-ounce) salmon fillets

2 teaspoons finely grated lime rind

155g (5 ounces) green beans, trimmed, chopped coarsely

1 cup (120g) frozen peas

⅓ cup finely chopped fresh mint

½ cup (125ml) buttermilk

1 tablespoon lime juice

1 Rub salmon all over with rind; season well. Cook salmon on a heated oiled grill plate (or grill or barbecue) until browned both sides and almost cooked through.
2 Meanwhile, boil, steam or microwave beans and peas, separately, until tender; drain. Combine beans, peas and half the mint in a medium bowl; season to taste.
3 Combine buttermilk, juice and remaining mint in a small jug; season to taste.
4 Serve fish with bean mixture; drizzle with buttermilk dressing.

prep + cook time 25 minutes **serves** 4
nutritional count per serving 11.9g total fat
(2.9g saturated fat); 1129kJ (270 cal);
4.7g carbohydrate; 34.4g protein; 3.1g fibre

fish skewers with lime, ginger and rocket

750g (1½ pounds) firm white fish fillets

1 tablespoon sesame oil

2 teaspoons finely grated lime rind

2 tablespoons lime juice

3 limes, extra, cut into wedges

60g (2 ounces) baby rocket (arugula)

2 tablespoons thinly sliced pickled ginger

1 tablespoon ginger pickling liquid

2 tablespoons kecap manis

1 Cut fish into 2.5cm (1 inch) pieces. Combine fish, oil, rind and juice in a large bowl.

2 Thread fish and lime wedges onto 12 skewers; season.

3 Preheat oiled grill plate (or grill or barbecue); cook skewers until browned all over and fish is just cooked through.

4 Combine rocket, ginger, ginger liquid and kecap manis in a small bowl; season. Serve skewers with salad.

prep + cook time 35 minutes **serves** 4
nutritional count per serving 18.1g total fat
(3.3g saturated fat); 1359kJ (325 cal);
1.1g carbohydrate; 39.3g protein; 0.5g fibre

tips We used swordfish steaks in this recipe, but any firm white fish fillet will be fine. Cover the ends of the bamboo skewers in foil to prevent them from burning during cooking. Pickled ginger can be either pink or red coloured and is available from Asian food shops. The paper-thin shavings of ginger are pickled in a mixture of vinegar, sugar and natural colouring.

Marinate the chicken overnight, if you can, for the best flavour. Prepare the ingredients for the salad, but combine them just before serving.

barbecued chicken with minted tomato salad

2 tablespoons lemon juice

1 tablespoon sumac

2 teaspoons finely chopped fresh oregano

2 tablespoons olive oil

6 x 200g (6½-ounce) chicken breast fillets

3 medium lemons (420g), halved

3 large pitta breads (240g)

minted tomato salad

2 tablespoons lemon juice

2 tablespoons olive oil

500g (1 pound) grape tomatoes, halved

2 lebanese cucumbers (260g), cut into ribbons

1 cup firmly packed fresh flat-leaf parsley leaves

1 cup firmly packed fresh mint leaves

2 teaspoons finely chopped fresh oregano

8 green onions (scallions), sliced thinly

1 Combine juice, sumac, oregano and half the oil in a large bowl with chicken. Stand for 10 minutes.

2 Season chicken; cook chicken on barbecue (or grill or grill plate) until browned both sides and cooked through. Stand for 5 minutes then slice thickly.

3 Meanwhile, make minted tomato salad.

4 Cook lemon, cut-side down, for 3 minutes or until browned lightly. Brush the bread on both sides with the remaining oil; brown lightly on barbecue, then break into coarse pieces.

5 Combine salad and bread; serve with chicken and lemon.

minted tomato salad Whisk juice and oil in a large serving bowl; add remaining ingredients, toss gently to combine. Season to taste.

prep + cook time 35 minutes **serves** 6
nutritional count per serving 24.4g total fat (5.2g saturated fat); 2199kJ (526 cal); 25.6g carbohydrate; 48.2g protein; 5.4g fibre

lamb and eggplant pitta pizza

200g (6½ ounces) lamb backstrap

½ teaspoon sumac

1 teaspoon ground allspice

1 tablespoon olive oil

4 pitta pocket breads (320g)

150g (4½ ounces) sliced char-grilled eggplant

⅓ cup (95g) bottled pizza sauce

2 cups (200g) pizza cheese

2 tablespoons hummus

2 tablespoons crème fraîche

½ medium red onion (85g), sliced thinly

½ cup loosely packed fresh coriander leaves (cilantro)

1 Heat oiled grill pan (or grill plate or barbecue).

2 Combine lamb, spices and oil in a medium bowl; season. Cook lamb for 5 minutes each side or until cooked as desired. Remove from heat; cover, rest for 10 minutes, then slice thinly.

3 Meanwhile, preheat grill (broiler). Place pitta pockets on an oiled oven tray; grill, one side only, until browned lightly. Remove from grill. (Keep grill on.)

4 Thickly slice eggplant. Spread untoasted side of pitta pockets with sauce; sprinkle with cheese and top with eggplant. Cook under grill for 5 minutes or until cheese is melted and browned lightly and eggplant is heated through.

5 Combine hummus and crème fraîche in a small bowl. Top pizzas with lamb, hummus mixture, onion and coriander.

prep + cook time 15 minutes **makes** 4
nutritional count per pizza 25.8g total fat
(11.9g saturated fat); 2487kJ (595 cal);
48.6g carbohydrate; 38.9g protein; 6.2g fibre

serving suggestion Green leafy salad.

pan-fries

A healthy way to cook, as pan-frying only uses a small amount of oil. For best results, pat the meat and vegies dry before frying.

greek-style pork fillet

1 tablespoon olive oil

½ cup (125ml) lemon juice

2 tablespoons dried oregano leaves

2 tablespoons dried parsley leaves

2 pork fillets (500g)

green beans with tomato

1 tablespoon olive oil

1 small brown onion (80g), sliced thinly

2 cloves garlic, sliced thinly

350g (11 ounces) green beans, trimmed

¼ cup (60ml) chicken stock

125g (4 ounces) cherry tomatoes, halved

2 tablespoons fresh flat-leaf parsley leaves

1 Make green beans with tomato.

2 Meanwhile, heat oil in a medium frying pan.

3 Toss juice, dried herbs and pork in a medium bowl; season. Drain pork; cook over high heat for 3 minutes each side. Cover, then cook a further 6 minutes or until cooked through. Remove from heat; stand for 5 minutes then slice pork thickly.

4 Serve pork with bean and tomato mixture.

green beans with tomato Heat oil in a medium saucepan over medium-high heat. Cook onion and garlic, stirring, for 5 minutes or until onion softens. Add beans and stock; cook, stirring occasionally, for 5 minutes or until vegetables soften. Add tomato; cook until heated through. Season to taste; sprinkle with fresh parsley to serve.

prep + cook time 35 minutes **serves** 4
nutritional count per serving 12.4g total fat
(2.3g saturated fat); 1100kJ (263 cal);
5g carbohydrate; 30.2g protein; 3.4g fibre

serving suggestion Serve with lemon rice: heat two 250g (8-ounce) packets of microwave rice according to packet directions. Combine in a large bowl with the finely grated rind of 1 lemon; season to taste.

honey mustard lamb cutlets

1 tablespoon dijon mustard

1 tablespoon wholegrain mustard

2 tablespoons honey

1 tablespoon white wine vinegar

12 french-trimmed lamb cutlets (600g)

400g (12½ ounces) green beans, trimmed

1 Combine mustards, honey and vinegar in a small jug. Toss half the honey mixture in a large bowl with cutlets.

2 Cook cutlets in a heated oiled large frying pan over medium heat until cooked as desired.

3 Boil, steam or microwave beans until tender; drain.

4 Serve cutlets with green beans; drizzle with remaining honey mixture.

prep + cook time 10 minutes **serves** 4

nutritional count per serving 13.2g total fat
(5.9g saturated fat); 1058kJ (253 cal);
4.5g carbohydrate; 17.7g protein; 2.9g fibre

serving suggestion Mashed potato, sweet potato or pumpkin.

tip Don't have the heat too high when cooking the cutlets as the honey will burn.

tips Japanese breadcrumbs, also known as panko is available in most major supermarkets and Asian food stores; you can use stale white or packaged breadcrumbs instead. Use a mandoline or V-slicer with a julienne attachment to cut the carrots into thin strips. Leftover chicken is delicious served with mayonnaise and lettuce on bread rolls.

lemon and thyme chicken schnitzel with coleslaw

2 tablespoons lemon juice

¼ cup (60ml) olive oil

2 teaspoons fresh thyme leaves

2 teaspoons bottled crushed garlic

650g (1¼ pounds) chicken tenderloins

¼ medium wombok (napa cabbage) (250g), shredded coarsely

1 large carrot (180g), cut into thin strips

¾ cup loosely packed fresh flat-leaf parsley leaves

⅓ cup (55g) dried currants

¼ cup (40g) pine nuts

1½ cups (115g) japanese breadcrumbs (panko)

vegetable oil, for shallow-frying

⅓ cup (100g) aïoli

lemon cheeks or wedges, to serve

1 Combine juice, oil, thyme and garlic in a small jug. Combine chicken and half the juice mixture in a large bowl.

2 To make coleslaw: combine cabbage, carrot, parsley, currants, nuts and remaining juice mixture in a medium bowl; season.

3 Place breadcrumbs in another large bowl; season. Heat vegetable oil in a large frying pan over medium-high heat.

4 Working in batches, lift chicken out of lemon mixture, drain off liquid, then toss in breadcrumbs to coat. Shallow-fry chicken pieces until browned lightly and cooked through. Drain on absorbent paper. Repeat with remaining chicken mixture and breadcrumbs.

5 Serve chicken with coleslaw and aïoli; accompany with lemon cheeks.

prep + cook time 30 minutes **serves** 4
nutritional count per serving 51.9g total fat (7.3g saturated fat); 3246kJ (776 cal); 31.5g carbohydrate; 44g protein; 5.6g fibre

dukkah-crusted lamb cutlets with cauliflower and baba ghanoush

1 small cauliflower (1kg)

¼ cup (60ml) olive oil

¼ cup (20g) natural sliced almonds

½ medium lemon (70g)

cooking-oil spray

⅓ cup (45g) dukkah

12 french-trimmed lamb cutlets (600g)

½ cup (100g) baba ghanoush

1 tablespoon fresh flat-leaf parsley leaves

1 tablespoon fresh mint leaves

lemon wedges, to serve

1 Preheat grill (broiler).

2 Trim cauliflower; cut into 1.5cm (¾-inch) thick slices. Place on an oven tray; drizzle with half the oil, season. Grill cauliflower for 8 minutes, turning halfway through cooking time, or until tender. Sprinkle with nuts; grill for 20 seconds or until nuts are browned lightly. Remove from grill; squeeze lemon juice over cauliflower.

3 Meanwhile, spray a large frying pan with oil; heat over medium-high heat.

4 Place dukkah in a shallow bowl. Rub remaining oil over lamb, season; press lamb firmly into dukkah to coat on both sides. Cook lamb for 3 minutes each side or until cooked as desired.

5 Serve lamb with cauliflower and baba ghanoush; sprinkle with herbs. Accompany with lemon wedges, and kumara crisps, if you like (see tip).

prep + cook time 20 minutes **serves** 4
nutritional count per serving 28.7g total fat
(6.3g saturated fat); 1652kJ (395 cal);
6.9g carbohydrate; 24.8g protein; 7.5g fibre

tip   To make the kumara (orange sweet potato) crisps, heat oil in a large frying pan over high heat until hot. Using a vegetable peeler, slice kumara into thin strips. Shallow-fry kumara, in batches, in hot oil until crisp. Drain on absorbent kitchen paper.

lamb cutlets with chips and lemon aïoli

800g (1½ pounds) frozen potato chips

12 french-trimmed lamb cutlets (600g)

1 teaspoon ground cumin

2 teaspoons ground coriander

½ teaspoon paprika

2 tablespoons lemon juice

1 tablespoon olive oil

lemon sprinkle

1 wedge preserved lemon rind

1 small clove garlic, chopped finely

¼ cup small fresh coriander leaves (cilantro)

¼ cup small fresh mint leaves

lemon aïoli

1 piece preserved lemon rind

½ cup (150g) store-bought aïoli

2 teaspoons lemon juice

1 Preheat oven to 200°C/400°F.

2 Cook chips following directions on packet.

3 Meanwhile, sprinkle lamb on both sides with combined cumin, coriander and paprika; drizzle with juice. Season.

4 Heat oil in a large frying pan over medium heat; cook cutlets for 2 minutes each side or until cooked as desired. Cover to keep warm.

5 Meanwhile, make lemon sprinkle and lemon aïoli.

6 Serve lamb with chips, lemon aïoli and topped with lemon sprinkle.

lemon sprinkle Discard flesh from preserved lemon rind; rinse rind under running water, pat dry. Finely chop rind; combine in a small bowl with remaining ingredients.

lemon aïoli Discard flesh from preserved lemon rind; rinse rind under running water, pat dry. Finely chop rind; combine in a small bowl with aïoli and juice.

prep + cook time 35 minutes **serves** 4

nutritional count per serving 56g total fat (11.2g saturated fat); 4366kJ (1043 cal); 94.5g carbohydrate; 26g protein; 9.8g fibre

serving suggestion Leafy green salad.

tip Preserved lemon rind is a North African specialty; the lemons are quartered and preserved in salt and lemon juice or water. To use, remove and discard the pulp; squeeze the juice from the rind, then rinse the rind well and slice thinly. It is sold in jars or singly by delicatessens; once opened, store in the fridge. It is also available from most major supermarkets.

tip If you can't find chicken minute steaks or uncrumbed schnitzels, cut 4 chicken breast fillets in half horizontally to make 8 fillets.

marsala chicken with bean puree

1 tablespoon olive oil

8 x 90g (3-ounce) chicken minute steaks

⅔ cup (160ml) marsala

¼ cup (60ml) water

¼ cup (60ml) pouring cream

white bean puree

800g (1½ pounds) canned cannellini beans, rinsed, drained

¼ cup (60ml) lemon juice

1 clove garlic, peeled

1 Heat oil in a large frying pan over high heat. Cook chicken, in batches, for 2 minutes each side or until golden brown and just cooked through. Remove from pan; cover to keep warm.
2 Add marsala and the water to frying pan; cook, stirring, for 3 minutes or until liquid is reduced by half. Add cream; cook, stirring occasionally, for 2 minutes or until mixture is reduced and thickened. Season to taste.
3 Meanwhile, make white bean puree.
4 Serve chicken and white bean puree with marsala sauce.

white bean puree Blend or process beans with juice and garlic until smooth. Transfer to a medium saucepan; cook bean mixture until warmed through. Season to taste.

prep + cook time 30 minutes **serves** 4
nutritional count per serving 13.4g total fat (5.3g saturated fat); 1878kJ (449 cal); 19.6g carbohydrate; 49.2g protein; 7.1g fibre

serving suggestion Roasted truss tomatoes and steamed greens – use a mixture of asparagus, beans and broccolini.

MASH

capsicum mash

Quarter 2 medium red capsicums; discard seeds and
membranes. Roast under a hot grill, skin-side up, until skin
blisters and blackens. Cover capsicum with plastic or paper for
5 minutes, then peel away skin. Blend capsicum until smooth.
Meanwhile, boil, steam or microwave 1kg (2lb) coarsely chopped
peeled potatoes until tender, drain. Mash potato; stir in ½ cup
hot pouring cream and 20g (¾oz) softened butter. Add capsicum;
stir until combined. Season to taste.

prep + cook time 30 minutes **serves** 4
nutritional count per serving 18g total fat (11.6g saturated fat);
1446kJ (346 cal); 36.2g carbohydrate; 7.7g protein; 4.7g fibre

potato mash

Place 1kg (2lb) coarsely chopped peeled potatoes in a medium
saucepan; add enough cold water to barely cover potato. Boil,
over medium heat, for 15 minutes or until potato is tender; drain.
Using the back of a wooden spoon, push potato through a fine
sieve into a large bowl. Stir 40g (1½oz) butter and ¾ cup hot milk
into potato, folding gently until mash is smooth and fluffy.

prep + cook time 30 minutes **serves** 4
nutritional count per serving 10.2g total fat (6.6g saturated fat);
991kJ (237 cal); 28.4g carbohydrate; 6.4g protein; 3.2g fibre

kumara mash

Boil, steam or microwave 500g (1lb) coarsely chopped peeled kumara and 500g (1lb) coarsely chopped peeled potatoes together until tender; drain. Mash in a large heatproof bowl. Combine ¼ cup chicken stock and 40g (1½oz) butter in a small saucepan over medium high heat until butter is melted. Stir into kumara mixture until combined. Season to taste.

prep + cook time 30 minutes **serves** 4
nutritional count per serving 8.5g total fat (5.4g saturated fat); 1024kJ (245 cal); 34.2g carbohydrate; 5.6g protein; 4.3g fibre

pumpkin mash

Boil, steam or microwave 500g (1lb) coarsely chopped peeled pontiac potatoes and 500g (1lb) coarsely chopped peeled pumpkin together until tender; drain. Mash potato and pumpkin; stir in 30g (1oz) butter. Season to taste.

prep + cook time 30 minutes **serves** 4
nutritional count per serving 6.5g total fat (2.6g saturated fat); 800kJ (191 cal); 25.6g carbohydrate; 4.7g protein; 5.3g fibre

tips Lamb noisette is a round, rather thick, cut of meat taken from the loin. We used a basil pesto dip from the refrigerated section of supermarkets, but you can use any pesto you like. Some major supermarkets and greengrocers are now selling bunches of baby carrots of different colours. We used a bunch each of orange, yellow and purple baby carrots. If you can't find the different colours, orange baby carrots will be fine.

prosciutto-wrapped lamb with mint pesto

4 lamb fillet noisettes (600g)

200g (6½ ounces) prosciutto

1 tablespoon olive oil

3 bunches baby carrots (1.2kg)

2 tablespoons honey

1 tablespoon fresh rosemary leaves

1 cup loosely packed fresh mint leaves

200g (6½-ounce) tub chunky basil pesto dip (see tips)

1 Season lamb; wrap in prosciutto. Heat oil in a large frying pan over medium-high heat. Cook lamb for 5 minutes each side or until cooked as desired. Remove from pan; cover lamb to keep warm.
2 Meanwhile, trim and peel carrots. Boil, steam or microwave carrots until just tender; toss through honey and rosemary.
3 Coarsely chop mint, stir through pesto; season to taste.
4 Serve lamb with carrots and pesto.

prep + cook time 20 minutes **serves** 4
nutritional count per serving 34g total fat
(7.3g saturated fat); 2785kJ (665 cal);
28.7g carbohydrate; 57.1g protein; 11.4g fibre

serving suggestion Leafy salad and crusty bread.

veal cutlets with polenta and sage tomatoes

2 cups (500ml) chicken stock

2 cups (500ml) milk

1 cup (170g) instant polenta

¾ cup (60g) finely grated parmesan

¼ cup (60ml) olive oil

4 veal cutlets (500g)

¼ cup loosely packed fresh sage leaves

250g (8 ounces) cherry truss tomatoes

2 tablespoons finely grated parmesan, extra

1 Bring stock and milk to the boil in a large saucepan; gradually add polenta. Reduce heat; simmer, stirring constantly, for 8 minutes or until polenta thickens. Stir in parmesan; season to taste.

2 Preheat grill (broiler). Heat half the oil in a large frying pan over high heat.

3 Season veal; press 2 sage leaves onto the side of each cutlet; cook veal for 3 minutes each side or until cooked as desired. Remove from pan, cover; stand 5 minutes.

4 Meanwhile, combine tomatoes and the remaining sage leaves and oil in a small baking dish; season. Grill for 5 minutes or until tomato skins burst.

5 Serve veal with polenta and sage tomatoes; sprinkle with extra parmesan.

prep + cook time 25 minutes **serves** 4
nutritional count per serving 28g total fat
(10.2g saturated fat); 2384kJ (570 cal);
37.6g carbohydrate; 40.8g protein; 2.2g fibre

serving suggestion Leafy green salad or steamed asparagus.

crumbed veal with capers and sage

8 x 100g (3-ounce) veal schnitzels

½ cup (80g) packaged coating mix

80g (2½ ounce) butter

¼ cup firmly packed fresh sage leaves

2 tablespoons rinsed, drained baby capers

1 teaspoon ground nutmeg

1 tablespoon lemon juice

lemon wedges, to serve

1 Coat veal in coating mix; shake off excess. Melt half the butter in a large frying pan over medium heat. Cook veal, in batches, for 2 minutes or until browned on both sides. Cover to keep warm.

2 Melt remaining butter in same pan. Add sage, capers and nutmeg; cook until sage is fragrant and slightly wilted. Return veal to pan with lemon juice. Toss to coat; cook until heated through. Serve veal with sauce; accompany with lemon wedges.

prep + cook time 15 minutes **serves** 4
nutritional count per serving 22.7g total fat
(12.5g saturated fat); 2508kJ (599 cal);
14.2g carbohydrate; 83.2g protein; 0.3g fibre

serving suggestion Mashed potato and garlicky green beans.

tip Packaged coating mix is a dried mixture of breadcrumbs and seasonings used to coat meat before frying. You can find it near the breadcrumbs in the seasonings and gravy aisle.

tips To flip the quesadillas, invert the frying pan with the quesadilla onto a plate, then slide the quesadilla back into the pan. Quesadillas can also be cooked in a sandwich press.

chicken quesadillas with avocado salad

2 cups loosely packed fresh coriander leaves (cilantro), chopped coarsely

2 fresh long green chillies, chopped coarsely

2 green onions (scallions), chopped coarsely

⅓ cup (80ml) lime juice

⅓ cup (80ml) olive oil

2 tablespoons water

1 barbecued chicken (900g)

8 x 20cm (8-inch) flour tortillas

3 cups (300g) pizza cheese

1 large avocado (320g)

2 large tomatoes (440g), chopped coarsely

2 fresh small red thai (serrano) chillies, chopped finely

1 To make salsa, blend or process coriander, chilli, onion, juice, oil and the water until finely chopped. Season to taste.

2 Heat a large oiled frying pan over medium heat.

3 Coarsely shred chicken, discard bones. Spread salsa over half of each tortilla; top with chicken and cheese. Fold tortillas in half; press down firmly.

4 Cook quesadillas in a heated frying pan, one at a time, for 1 minute each side or until browned lightly; wrap in foil to keep warm. Repeat with remaining quesadillas.

5 Meanwhile, slice avocado into wedges; slice wedges in half widthways. Toss avocado, tomato and chilli in a medium bowl to combine; season to taste.

6 Cut each quesadilla into four wedges; serve with remaining salsa and avocado salad.

prep + cook time 25 minutes **serves** 4
nutritional count per serving 59.5g total fat
(19g saturated fat); 4598kJ (1098 cal);
38.9g carbohydrate; 99g protein; 6g fibre

serving suggestion Toss some rinsed, drained corn kernels through the avocado salad, if you like; accompany with a green leafy salad.

chicken and leek free-form pastries

1 sheet puff pastry

2 tablespoons olive oil

8 chicken tenderloins (600g)

20g (¾ ounce) butter

1 teaspoon bottled crushed garlic

1 small leek (200g), sliced thinly

4 shortcut bacon slices (140g), chopped finely

1 tablespoon dijon mustard

¼ cup (60ml) dry white wine

¾ cup (180ml) thickened (heavy) cream

1 Preheat oven to 200°C/400°F.

2 Cut pastry into 4 squares; place on an oiled oven tray. Bake 15 minutes or until browned lightly and crisp.

3 Meanwhile, heat oil in a large frying pan over high heat. Coarsely chop chicken; cook chicken, in batches, until browned.

4 Add butter, garlic, leek and bacon to pan; cook, stirring, until leek softens. Stir in mustard and wine; bring to the boil. Reduce heat; simmer, uncovered, 2 minutes or until reduced by half. Stir in cream; simmer, uncovered, until sauce thickens slightly. Season to taste.

5 To serve, top chicken mixture with pastry squares.

prep + cook time 20 minutes **serves** 4
nutritional count per serving 45.1g total fat
(17.6g saturated fat); 2788kJ (667 cal);
18g carbohydrate; 44.7g protein; 1.7g fibre

serving suggestion Mashed potato and rocket leaves.
tip Tubs of mashed potato are available from the refrigerated section of most larger supermarkets – just heat in the microwave, following the directions on the tub, and serve.

oven-baked

There's something quite comforting about food that's been baked or roasted, but that doesn't mean it has to be time-consuming.

tip You can cook your own rice, if you like (cook 1½ cups basmati rice following the absorption method directions on the packet). You can use chicken thigh cutlets (1.2kg/2½ pounds) instead of the marylands.

tandoori chicken with pomegranate raita

¼ cup (75g) tandoori paste

4 small chicken marylands (1.2kg)

2 tablespoons yoghurt

500g (1 pound) packet microwavable basmati rice

pomegranate raita

1 cup (280g) yoghurt

2 teaspoons finely grated lime rind

1 tablespoon lime juice

⅓ cup (80ml) pomegranate seeds

lime cheeks or wedges, to serve

1 Preheat oven to 220°C/425°F.

2 Combine tandoori paste, chicken and yoghurt in a large bowl; season. Cook chicken on a heated oiled grill plate over high heat for 5 minutes or until browned; place on a baking-paper-lined baking tray. Cover chicken; transfer to oven, bake for 20 minutes or until cooked through.

3 Meanwhile, heat rice according to directions on packet.

4 Make pomegranate raita. Serve chicken with rice, pomegranate raita and lime cheeks.

pomegranate raita Combine yoghurt, rind, juice and half the pomegranate seeds in a small bowl. Sprinkle with remaining seeds to serve.

prep + cook time 35 minutes **serves** 4
nutritional count per serving 18.4g total fat (6.7g saturated fat); 2849kJ (681 cal); 76.4g carbohydrate; 49.2g protein; 1.9g fibre

serving suggestion Tomato, onion and cucumber salad or baby spinach salad.

chicken curry pot pies

1 tablespoon vegetable oil

800g (1½ pounds) chicken thigh fillets, chopped coarsely

2 tablespoons korma curry paste

1 cup (125g) frozen peas

1 tablespoon cornflour (cornstarch)

1½ cups (375ml) chicken stock

1 tablespoon finely chopped fresh coriander (cilantro)

1 sheet frozen puff pastry, thawed

1 egg, beaten lightly

1 Preheat oven to 200°C/400°F. Grease four 1-cup (250ml) 10cm x 6cm (4-inch x 2½-inch) ovenproof ramekins. Place on a baking tray.

2 Heat oil in a large frying pan over high heat; cook chicken, stirring, until browned all over and cooked through. Add curry paste; cook, stirring, until fragrant. Add peas and combined cornflour and stock; bring to the boil. Reduce heat; simmer, stirring, until sauce has thickened. Stir in coriander; season.

3 Divide mixture evenly between ramekins. Cut pastry into quarters. Press one pastry square over the top of each ramekin; brush with egg. Bake 15 minutes or until pastry is browned lightly and puffed.

prep + cook time 35 minutes **serves** 4
nutritional count per serving 57.8g total fat (18.9g saturated fat); 3201kJ (765 cal); 24.2g carbohydrate; 38.1g protein; 3.1g fibre

serving suggestion Tomato and rocket salad.

tip The chicken pie filling can be made a day ahead. Heat until warm then add the pastry and bake just before serving.You can brush the pastry with a little milk instead of the egg, if preferred.

tuna and corn bake

200g (6½ ounces) rigatoni pasta

45g (1½ ounces) butter

1½ tablespoons plain (all-purpose) flour

2½ cups (625ml) hot milk

1½ cups (180g) coarsely grated cheddar

420g (13½ ounces) canned corn kernels, rinsed, drained

425g (13½ ounces) canned tuna in springwater, drained, flaked

1 cup (120g) frozen peas

2 green onions (scallions), chopped finely

2 tablespoons finely chopped fresh flat-leaf parsley

2 tablespoons lemon juice

1 Preheat oven to 220°C/425°F.

2 Cook pasta in a large saucepan of boiling water until tender; drain.

3 Meanwhile, melt butter in a medium saucepan. Add flour; cook, stirring, for 1 minute or until mixture bubbles and thickens. Gradually stir in milk; cook, stirring, until sauce boils and thickens. Stir in pasta, ⅓ cup of the cheese, corn, tuna, peas, onion, parsley and juice; season to taste.

4 Spoon mixture into a 2-litre (8-cup) ovenproof dish; sprinkle with remaining cheese. Bake, uncovered, for 20 minutes or until browned lightly.

prep + cook time 40 minutes **serves** 6
nutritional count per serving 22.8g total fat
(13.9g saturated fat); 2103kJ (503 cal);
41.2g carbohydrate; 31.2g protein; 4.5g fibre

serving suggestion Mixed salad and crusty bread.

tips The recipe can be made several hours ahead to the end of step 3. Add another ½ cup milk if making ahead as the sauce will thicken on standing. From cold, bake, covered, at 200°C/400°F for 30 minutes or until heated through then uncover and bake for a further 10 minutes or until browned.

tip You can use the chopped meat from one barbecued chicken in this recipe instead of the tenderloins. Add it at the end of step 4 and stir until hot. Recipe can be made several hours ahead to the end of step 5. From cold, bake, covered, at 200°C/400°F for 30 minutes or until heated through then uncover and bake for a further 10 minutes or until browned.

cheesy chicken, tomato and bacon rigatoni

315g (10 ounces) rigatoni pasta

2 tablespoons olive oil

500g (1 pound) chicken tenderloins, sliced thinly

1 medium red onion (170g), sliced thinly

4 rindless bacon slices (260g), chopped coarsely

2 cups (500g) bottled tomato pasta sauce

¼ cup finely chopped fresh basil

1½ cups (180g) coarsely grated cheddar

fresh basil, extra

1 Preheat oven to 220°C/425°F.

2 Cook pasta in a large saucepan of boiling water until tender; drain. Return to pan.

3 Meanwhile, heat half the oil in a large frying pan over high heat; cook chicken until browned. Remove from pan.

4 Heat remaining oil in same pan; cook onion and bacon, stirring, until bacon is crisp. Return chicken to pan with sauce; simmer, uncovered, for 10 minutes. Stir in basil; season to taste.

5 Stir chicken mixture and half the cheese into pasta. Spoon pasta mixture into a 2-litre (8-cup) ovenproof dish; sprinkle with remaining cheese.

6 Bake, uncovered, for 10 minutes or until mixture is browned lightly. Sprinkle with extra basil to serve.

prep + cook time 40 minutes **serves** 4
nutritional count per serving 34.9g total fat
(14g saturated fat); 3540kJ (847 cal);
65.8g carbohydrate; 64g protein; 6g fibre

serving suggestion Leafy green salad or steamed asparagus.

cheese parcels with tomato and olive salad

200g (6 ounces) soft ricotta

200g (6 ounces) soft fetta

⅔ cup (160g) sour cream

2 eggs

8 sheets fillo pastry

cooking-oil spray

2 lebanese cucumbers (260g), sliced finely

250g (8 ounces) cherry tomatoes, halved

½ cup (60g) pitted black olives, halved

½ cup loosely packed fresh mint leaves

½ cup loosely packed fresh flat-leaf parsley leaves

1 tablespoon red wine vinegar

2 tablespoons olive oil

1 Preheat oven to 200°C/400°F. Line an oven tray with baking paper.

2 Mix cheeses, sour cream and eggs in a small bowl until smooth; season.

3 Layer pastry sheets on board, spraying with oil between layers. Cut pastry stack in half crossways into two pieces. Shape half the cheese mixture into a log on one pastry stack, leaving a 3cm (1¼-inch) border at bottom and sides. Fold in sides, then roll pastry tightly over filling to enclose. Spray with oil; place, seam-side down, on oven tray. Repeat with remaining pastry stack and cheese mixture.

4 Bake parcels for 5 minutes or until browned.

5 Meanwhile, combine cucumber, tomato, olives and herbs in a medium bowl with vinegar and oil. Season to taste.

6 Cut parcels in half; serve with salad.

prep + cook time 20 minutes **serves** 4
nutritional count per serving 50.8g total fat
(24.6g saturated fat); 2660kJ (636 cal);
20.7g carbohydrate; 22.6g protein; 4.3g fibre

tip Parcels can be made several hours ahead. Reheat just before serving.

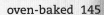

tip The kumara mixture can be roasted and the pasta cooked several hours ahead. Assemble close to serving. From cold, bake, covered, at 200°C/400°F for 30 minutes or until heated through then uncover and bake for a further 10 minutes or until browned.

baked penne with kumara and spinach

2 medium red onions (340g), cut into wedges

2 small kumara (orange sweet potato) (600g), sliced thickly

2 tablespoons olive oil

375g (12 ounces) penne pasta

250g (8 ounces) frozen spinach, thawed, drained

1½ cups (360g) soft ricotta

1 clove garlic, crushed

¼ cup (60ml) pouring cream

800g (1½ pounds) canned crushed tomatoes

¼ cup (40g) pine nuts

½ cup (40g) finely grated parmesan

1 Preheat oven to 240°C/475°F.
2 Combine onion, kumara and oil in a large baking dish; season. Roast, uncovered, stirring once, for 25 minutes or until vegetables are tender.
3 Meanwhile, cook pasta in a large saucepan of boiling water until just tender; drain.
4 Combine pasta in a large bowl with spinach, ricotta, garlic, cream and tomatoes; season.
5 Spread kumara mixture over the base of a 3-litre (12-cup) baking dish. Top with pasta mixture; sprinkle with nuts and parmesan. Bake, covered, for 5 minutes. Uncover; bake for a further 5 minutes or until browned.

prep + cook time 40 minutes **serves** 6
nutritional count per serving 25.3g total fat (9.8g saturated fat); 2450kJ (586 cal); 63.4g carbohydrate; 21.9g protein; 8.4g fibre

salmon and potato parcels

1 tablespoon olive oil

1 medium brown onion (150g), chopped finely

2 cloves garlic, crushed

400g (12½ ounces) canned crushed tomatoes

1 tablespoon coarsely chopped fresh flat-leaf parsley

1 tablespoon coarsely chopped fresh mint

4 baby new potatoes (chats) (160g), sliced thinly

4 x 220g (7-ounce) skinless salmon fillets

1 medium lemon (140g), sliced thinly

1 Preheat oven to 200°C/400°F.

2 Heat oil in a large frying pan; cook onion and garlic, stirring, until onion softens. Add tomatoes and herbs; bring to the boil. Reduce heat; simmer about 5 minutes or until mixture has thickened and reduced slightly. Season to taste.

3 Place potato, slightly overlapping, onto four 30cm x 40cm (12-inch x 16-inch) pieces of baking paper; top with salmon. Spoon tomato mixture over salmon; top with lemon. Fold paper to enclose fish.

4 Place parcels on a baking tray; bake about 15 minutes or until fish is cooked as desired. Serve fish in parcel.

prep + cook time 30 minutes **serves** 4
nutritional count per serving 28.4g total fat (6.9g saturated fat); 2222kJ (531 cal); 10.4g carbohydrate; 55.6g protein; 3.8g fibre

serving suggestion Preserved lemon and olive couscous.

tip To fold the parcel, bring long sides to meet in the middle, fold over about 1cm (½-inch) folding all the way down. Then fold edges under to enclose.

PIZZA

meat lovers' pizza

Preheat oven to 240°C/475°F. Oil two oven or pizza trays; place in heated oven. Heat 1 tablespoon olive oil in a large frying pan; cook 1 finely chopped medium brown onion until softened. Add 200g (6½oz) minced (ground) beef and 1 crushed garlic clove; cook, stirring, for 3 minutes or until beef is browned. Stir in 1 cup bottled tomato pasta sauce (passata); remove from heat, season. Place 2 x 30cm (12in) round pizza bases on trays, spread with beef mixture, sprinkle with 1 cup pizza cheese. Top with 6 halved large slices hot sopressa salami and 1 thickly sliced cured chorizo sausage. Bake pizzas about 15 minutes or until bases are browned and crisp.

prep + cook time 35 minutes **serves** 4
nutritional count per serving 37.4g total fat (13.1g saturated fat); 3235kJ (774 cal); 66.7g carbohydrate; 40.2g protein; 6.3g fibre

greek pizza

Preheat oven to 240°C/475°F. Oil one oven tray; place in heated oven for 5 minutes. Place 1 x 400g (12½oz) afghan bread on tray; spread with ¾ cup bottled tomato pasta sauce (passata). Top with 1 thinly sliced medium yellow or red capsicum (bell pepper), 155g (5oz) crumbled fetta, and ½ cup pitted black olives. Sprinkle with 1 teaspoon dried oregano; drizzle with 1 tablespoon olive oil, season. Bake pizza for 15 minutes or until base is browned and crisp.

prep + cook time 30 minutes **serves** 4
nutritional count per serving 18.7g total fat (7.2g saturated fat); 2161kJ (517 cal); 66g carbohydrate; 18.3g protein; 5.7g fibre

tip This pizza can also be made using 2 x 30cm (12in) round pizza bases instead of the afghan bread.

pepperoni pizza

Preheat oven to 240°C/475°F. Oil two oven or pizza trays; place in heated oven for 5 minutes. Place 2 x 30cm (12in) round pizza bases on trays, spread with 1 cup bottled arrabbiata pasta sauce; sprinkle with ½ cup of pizza cheese. Top with 125g (4oz) thinly sliced pepperoni and 1 thinly sliced small red capsicum (bell pepper); sprinkle with an extra 1 cup pizza cheese, season. Bake pizzas for 15 minutes or until bases are browned and crisp.

prep + cook time 30 minutes **serves** 4
nutritional count per serving 24.5g total fat (9.9g saturated fat); 2550kJ (610 cal); 65g carbohydrate; 29.4g protein; 5.9g fibre

barbecue chicken pizza

Preheat oven to 240°C/475°F. Oil two oven or pizza trays; place in heated oven for 5 minutes. Place 2 x 30cm (12in) round pizza bases on trays, spread with ⅓ cup barbecue sauce; top with 1½ cups shredded barbecued chicken, 1 thinly sliced small red onion and 1 thinly sliced flat mushroom. Sprinkle with ½ cup pizza cheese; season. Bake pizzas about 15 minutes or until bases are browned and crisp. Sprinkle with 2 tablespoons fresh flat-leaf parsley leaves

prep + cook time 35 minutes **serves** 4
nutritional count per serving 11.5g total fat (3.6g saturated fat); 2136kJ (511 cal); 70.5g carbohydrate; 28.5g protein; 5.7g fibre

tips You can use 1 cup thawed frozen corn kernels instead of canned, if you prefer. It is fine to use shredded barbecued chicken in this recipe. A large (900g/1¾-pound) chicken should give 3 cups of shredded chicken meat. Mexican is a popular cuisine, especially with children: cayenne pepper, however, is extremely hot so the amount used should be adjusted depending on whether you are cooking for adults or kids.

creamy chicken and corn burritos

1¼ cups loosely packed fresh coriander leaves (cilantro)

310g (10 ounces) canned corn kernels, rinsed, drained

3 cups (480g) shredded cooked chicken

2 cups (240g) coarsely grated cheddar

1 cup (240g) light sour cream

1 clove garlic, crushed

½ teaspoon cayenne pepper

8 x 20cm (8-inch) flour tortillas

lime wedges, to serve

1 Preheat oven to 220°C/425°F. Oil a large ovenproof dish.
2 Coarsely chop ¼ cup of the coriander. Combine chopped coriander, corn, chicken, 1 cup of the cheese, sour cream, garlic and cayenne in a medium bowl; season.
3 To make burritos, divide chicken mixture on centre of tortillas; roll tortillas to enclose filling, folding in sides. Place burritos in dish; sprinkle with remaining cheese.
4 Bake, uncovered, for 25 minutes or until browned lightly.
5 Sprinkle burritos with remaining coriander; serve with lime wedges.

prep + cook time 35 minutes serves 4
nutritional count per serving 46.6g total fat (24.3g saturated fat); 3532kJ (845 cal); 49g carbohydrate; 54.7g protein; 4.1g fibre

serving idea Tomato and avocado salad.

mexican chicken tortilla bake

1 tablespoon olive oil

1 large red onion (300g), sliced thinly

1 medium red capsicum (bell pepper) (200g),
sliced thinly

800g (1½ pounds) canned diced tomatoes

420g (13½ ounces) canned kidney beans, rinsed, drained

310g (10 ounces) canned corn kernels, rinsed, drained

35g (1-ounce) packet taco spice mix

2 cups (320g) shredded barbecued chicken

⅓ cup coarsely chopped fresh coriander (cilantro)

4 x 19cm (7½-inch) flour tortillas

¾ cup (75g) coarsely grated mozzarella

1 Preheat oven to 220°C/425°F.

2 Heat oil in a large saucepan over medium-high heat; cook onion and capsicum, stirring, until tender. Add tomatoes, beans, corn and seasoning; simmer, uncovered, for 10 minutes or until mixture thickens slightly. Add chicken and coriander; cook, stirring, until hot. Season to taste.

3 Line base and sides of a 20cm (8-inch) springform pan with foil or baking paper; place on an oven tray. Line base of pan with one tortilla; top with one-third of the chicken mixture. Repeat layering with remaining tortillas and chicken mixture, finishing with a tortilla; sprinkle with cheese. Bake, uncovered, for 20 minutes or until browned lightly. Stand for 5 minutes before cutting.

prep + cook time 40 minutes **serves** 6
nutritional count per serving 13.2g total fat
(3.9g saturated fat); 1572kJ (376 cal);
33.8g carbohydrate; 26.4g protein; 8.1g fibre

serving suggestion Avocado salad or guacamole.
tip You need to buy half a large barbecued chicken (450g) to get the amount of shredded meat required for this recipe.

honey and chilli soy chicken

1 fresh small red thai (serrano) chilli, sliced thinly

¼ cup (60ml) soy sauce

2 tablespoons honey

1 tablespoon sesame oil

¼ teaspoon sea salt flakes

3 cloves garlic, crushed

4 small chicken thigh cutlets (640g)

2 tablespoons peanut oil

1 medium brown onion (150g), sliced thinly

1 medium carrot (120g), sliced thinly lengthways

125g (4 ounces) baby corn, halved lengthways

½ wombok (napa cabbage) (200g), shredded

1 tablespoon oyster sauce

1 Preheat oven to 200°C/400°F.

2 Combine chilli, soy sauce, honey, sesame oil, salt, half the garlic and chicken in a large bowl.

3 Heat half the peanut oil in a large wok over high heat; stir-fry chicken, in batches, until just browned. Transfer chicken and juices to a baking-paper-lined oven tray. Bake, uncovered, for 20 minutes or until chicken is cooked through.

4 Heat remaining oil in wok. Add onion, carrot and remaining garlic; stir-fry until onion softens. Add corn; stir-fry for 2 minutes, add cabbage and oyster sauce; stir-fry for 1 minute or until cabbage is just wilted. Season to taste.

5 Serve stir-fried vegetables topped with chicken cutlets.

prep + cook time 35 minutes **serves** 4
nutritional count per serving 43.5g total fat
(11.3g saturated fat); 2537kJ (606 cal);
24.1g carbohydrate; 28.6g protein; 4.8g fibre

tips You can use a mandoline or V-slicer to slice the onion and shred the cabbage. Use the julienne attachment to thinly slice the carrots. If the chicken cutlets are large, you can make two or three deep cuts into the chicken to the bone to speed up the cooking time.

tip You can use japanese breadcrumbs (panko) in place of the stale breadcrumbs to save time. Substitute parmesan for the pecorino, if you prefer.

macaroni cheese

280g (9 ounces) macaroni

4 rindless bacon slices (260g), chopped finely

45g (1½ ounces) butter

⅓ cup (50g) plain (all-purpose) flour

1 litre (4 cups) milk

1 cup (120g) coarsely grated cheddar

½ cup (40g) finely grated pecorino cheese

2 tablespoons wholegrain (seeded) mustard

½ cup (35g) stale breadcrumbs

20g (¾ ounce) butter, extra

1 Preheat oven to 220°C/425°F. Oil a deep 2-litre (8-cup) ovenproof dish.
2 Cook pasta in a large saucepan of boiling water until just tender; drain.
3 Meanwhile, cook bacon in a heated medium saucepan, stirring, until crisp; drain on kitchen paper.
4 Melt butter in same pan, add flour; cook, stirring, for 1 minute. Gradually stir in milk; cook, stirring, until sauce boils and thickens. Cool for 2 minutes, then stir in cheeses and mustard; season to taste.
5 Combine pasta, cheese sauce and bacon in a large bowl; pour mixture into ovenproof dish. Top with breadcrumbs, dot with extra butter. Bake 15 minutes or until browned.

prep + cook time 40 minutes **serves** 4
nutritional count per serving 47.5g total fat (27.8g saturated fat); 3854kJ (922 cal); 78.8g carbohydrate; 43.1g protein; 3.5g fibre

tips You can add the chopped meat from one barbecued chicken instead of cooking the chicken breast – add it in step 4. The recipe can be made to the end of step 5 several hours ahead. From cold, bake, covered at 200°C/400°F for 30 minutes or until heated through then uncover and bake for a further 10 minutes or until browned.

creamy chicken, mushroom and asparagus bake

375g (12 ounces) rigatoni pasta

60g (2 ounces) butter

600g (1¼ pounds) chicken breast fillets, cut into 1cm (½ inch) pieces

100g (3 ounces) button mushrooms, sliced thinly

2 tablespoons plain (all-purpose) flour

2 cups (500ml) milk

½ cup (40g) coarsely grated romano

1¼ cups (150g) coarsely grated cheddar

170g (5½ ounces) asparagus, trimmed, chopped coarsely

¼ cup coarsely chopped fresh flat-leaf parsley

1 Preheat oven to 200°C/400°F.

2 Cook pasta in a large saucepan of boiling water until just tender; drain.

3 Meanwhile, heat a third of the butter in a large frying pan over medium-high heat; cook chicken, in batches, until browned and cooked through. Remove from pan.

4 Heat remaining butter in pan; cook mushrooms, stirring, until tender. Add flour; cook, stirring, 1 minute. Gradually stir in milk. Stir over medium heat until mixture boils and thickens. Stir in chicken, ¼ cup of the romano, ¾ cup of the cheddar and the asparagus. Season to taste.

5 Combine chicken mixture and drained pasta in a 2.5-litre (10-cup) ovenproof dish; sprinkle with remaining cheeses.

6 Bake, uncovered, for 15 minutes or until top browns lightly. Serve sprinkled with parsley.

prep + cook time 40 minutes **serves** 4
nutritional count per serving 37.3g total fat (22.3g saturated fat); 3775kJ (903 cal); 75.2g carbohydrate; 64g protein; 4.8g fibre

serving suggestion Tossed salad.

pea and salmon bake

375g (12 ounces) rigatoni pasta

30g (1 ounce) butter

2 tablespoons plain (all-purpose) flour

2 cups (500ml) milk

1½ cups (180g) frozen peas

½ cup (40g) coarsely grated parmesan

1¼ cups (150g) coarsely grated cheddar

415g (13 ounces) canned pink salmon, drained, skin and bones removed

1 Preheat oven to 200°C/400°F.

2 Cook pasta in a large saucepan of boiling water until just tender; drain.

3 Meanwhile, melt butter in a medium saucepan. Add flour; cook, stirring, until mixture thickens and bubbles. Gradually stir in milk; stir over medium heat until sauce boils and thickens. Stir in peas, ¼ cup parmesan and ¾ cup cheddar. Season to taste.

4 Combine sauce mixture with pasta and salmon in an oiled shallow 2.5-litre (10-cup) ovenproof dish; sprinkle with remaining combined cheeses.

5 Bake, uncovered, for 20 minutes or until browned lightly.

prep + cook time 35 minutes **serves** 6
nutritional count per serving 23.8g total fat
(13.7g saturated fat); 2345kJ (561 cal);
51.2g carbohydrate; 33.1g protein; 3.9g fibre

serving suggestion Steamed asparagus or broccoli or a green leafy salad.

tips You can use red salmon or canned tuna if you like. The recipe can be made to the end of step 4 several hours ahead. From cold, bake, covered at 200°C/400°F for 30 minutes or until heated through then uncover and bake for a further 10 minutes or until browned.

tips You can use minced (ground) beef, if you prefer. Recipe can be made to the end of step 5 several hours ahead. From cold, bake, covered, at 200°C/400°F for 30 minutes or until heated through then uncover and bake for a further 10 minutes or until browned.

baked bolognese pasta

2 tablespoons olive oil

1 medium brown onion (150g), chopped finely

1 medium carrot (120g), grated finely

1 clove garlic, crushed

500g (1 pound) minced (ground) pork and veal mixture

800g (1½ pounds) canned peeled chopped tomatoes

2 tablespoons tomato paste

½ cup (125ml) chicken stock or water

375g (12 ounces) small penne pasta

2 cups (480g) soft ricotta

1 cup (80g) coarsely grated parmesan

2 tablespoons olive oil, extra

1 Preheat oven to 240°C/475°F. Oil a 3-litre (12-cup) ovenproof dish.

2 Heat oil in a large saucepan over medium-high heat, add onion, carrot and garlic; cook, stirring, for 5 minutes or until onion softens. Add minced pork and veal mixture to pan; cook, stirring, until browned.

3 Stir tomatoes, paste and stock into pan; bring to the boil. Simmer, uncovered, for 5 minutes or until mixture thickens slightly. Season to taste.

4 Meanwhile, cook pasta in a large saucepan of boiling water until just tender; drain. Return pasta to pan; stir in meat mixture.

5 Pour pasta mixture into ovenproof dish. Combine ricotta and half the parmesan in a medium bowl; season. Spread over top of hot pasta mixture. Drizzle with extra oil. Top with remaining parmesan.

6 Bake for 10 minutes or until browned lightly.

prep + cook time 40 minutes **serves** 4
nutritional count per serving 48.7g total fat (19g saturated fat); 4172kJ (998 cal); 76.5g carbohydrate; 59.9g protein; 7.3g fibre

serving suggestion Green leafy salad.

moroccan roasted lamb racks

4 x 4 french-trimmed lamb cutlet racks (720g)

2 teaspoons ground allspice

½ teaspoon cayenne pepper

1 tablespoon olive oil

250g (8 ounces) baby vine-ripened truss tomatoes

cooking-oil spray

1 cup firmly packed fresh mint leaves

1 small red onion (100g), sliced thinly

1 tablespoon lemon juice

⅔ cup (160g) baba ghanoush

1 Preheat oven to 220°C/425°F.

2 Combine lamb, spices and oil in a large bowl; place lamb in a large shallow baking dish. Roast, uncovered, for 20 minutes or until cooked as desired. Cover; rest for 5 minutes.

3 After lamb has been in the oven for 10 minutes, add the tomatoes to the dish; spray with oil. Roast for 10 minutes or until the tomatoes soften.

4 Combine tomatoes with mint, onion and juice in a medium bowl. Serve lamb with tomato salad and baba ghanoush.

prep + cook time 40 minutes **serves** 6
nutritional count per serving 29.1g total fat (9.4g saturated fat); 1605kJ (384 cal); 5.3g carbohydrate; 23g protein; 8g fibre

tips Veal schnitzel is thinly sliced steak available crumbed or plain (uncrumbed). In this recipe we used plain schnitzel; they are also known as escalopes. We used a bottled cherry tomato arrabbiata pasta sauce – it has a chilli kick to it – but you can use any tomato pasta sauce you like.

veal and bocconcini stacks

440g (15 ounces) bocconcini

8 x 100g (3-ounce) veal schnitzels

24 sage leaves

8 slices prosciutto (120g)

700g (1½-pound) bottled tomato pasta sauce

1 cup (80g) finely grated parmesan

1 Preheat oven to 200°C/400°F.

2 Thinly slice bocconcini. Place four pieces of veal in an oiled medium shallow ovenproof dish; season. Top each with 3 sage leaves, 1 slice prosciutto, 2 slices bocconcini and another piece of veal. Repeat layering, ending with the bocconcini; you will have four stacks.

3 Pour sauce over veal stacks; sprinkle with parmesan. Cover dish with foil; bake for 20 minutes. Uncover; bake for a further 5 minutes or until browned lightly.

prep + cook time 35 minutes **serves** 4
nutritional count per serving 35.4g total fat (18.4g saturated fat); 3057kJ (731 cal); 19.9g carbohydrate; 80.8g protein; 5.7g fibre

serving suggestions Soft polenta and a leafy salad.
tips Use any left-over ingredients from this dish to make a delicious pizza topping. Spread the sauce over a store-bought pizza base, top with sliced bocconcini and coarsely chopped prosciutto if there's some left. Cook in a hot oven until the base is crisp, then top with sage leaves before serving.

salads

Once relegated to the status of a humble side dish, many salads now star as a filling, stand-alone main course meal.

pork chipolata and risoni salad

375g (12 ounces) risoni pasta

1 tablespoon olive oil

360g (11½ ounces) pork chipolata sausages

200g (6½ ounces) button mushrooms, halved

1 small red onion (100g), sliced thinly

⅔ cup (160g) roasted red capsicum (bell pepper) strips

100g (3 ounces) baby rocket (arugula)

¼ cup loosely packed fresh flat-leaf parsley

lemon dressing

¼ cup (60ml) lemon juice

1 clove garlic, crushed

⅓ cup (80ml) olive oil

1 Cook pasta in a large saucepan of boiling water until tender; drain. Rinse under cold running water; drain.
2 Make lemon dressing.
3 Heat half the oil in a large frying pan over high heat; cook chipolatas, turning occasionally, until cooked through. Remove from pan; cover to keep warm. Heat remaining oil in same frying pan; cook mushrooms, stirring, until browned.
4 Thickly slice chipolatas. Combine pasta, chipolatas, mushrooms, remaining ingredients and lemon dressing in a large bowl; toss to combine, season.

lemon dressing Place ingredients in a screw-top jar, shake well; season to taste.

prep + cook time 30 minutes **serves** 6
nutritional count per serving 22.3g total fat
(8g saturated fat); 2024kJ (483 cal);
49g carbohydrate; 19.1g protein; 5g fibre

tips Without the prawns, this salad would be a delicious side salad for barbecued beef, lamb or chicken. The recipe is best made close to serving.

crunchy snow pea, prawn and avocado salad

750g (1½ pounds) cooked medium king prawns (shrimp)

150g (4½ ounces) sugar snap peas, trimmed

3 small avocados (600g), sliced thickly

2 cups (100g) snow pea sprouts

chive vinaigrette

¼ cup (60ml) white wine vinegar

¼ cup (60ml) olive oil

¼ cup finely chopped fresh chives

1 Make chive vinaigrette.

2 Shell and devein prawns leaving tails intact.

3 Boil, steam or microwave peas until just tender; drain, rinse under cold water, drain.

4 Combine peas in a large bowl with prawns, avocado, sprouts and vinaigrette; toss gently. Season to taste.

chive vinaigrette Combine ingredients in a small bowl. Season to taste.

prep + cook time 25 minutes **serves** 4
nutritional count per serving 38.2g total fat
(7.2g saturated fat); 1998kJ (478 cal);
8.2g carbohydrate; 24.6g protein; 3.7g fibre

tips Farfalle is good for a dish such as this because the folds and crinkles in the pasta help capture the pesto and hold the other ingredients. Replace the farfalle with penne or small shells if you wish. Rocket pesto can be made 3 days ahead; refrigerate it with plastic wrap pressed onto the surface to prevent it discolouring.

poached salmon and pesto pasta salad

500g (1 pound) farfalle pasta

800g (1½ pounds) salmon fillets, skin and bones removed

1.25 litres (5 cups) water

½ medium lemon (70g), cut into wedges

1 small red onion (100g), sliced thinly

2 tablespoons rinsed, drained capers

2 medium tomatoes (300g), seeded, chopped finely

1 lebanese cucumber (130g), seeded, chopped finely

1 tablespoon finely grated lemon rind

⅓ cup (80ml) lemon juice

rocket pesto

250g (8 ounces) rocket (arugula), trimmed

¼ cup (20g) coarsely grated parmesan

¼ cup (40g) roasted pine nuts

2 cloves garlic, quartered

½ cup (125ml) olive oil

1 Make rocket pesto.

2 Meanwhile, cook pasta in a large saucepan of boiling water until just tender; drain.

3 Halve salmon fillets. Bring the water with the lemon wedges to the boil in a large frying pan. Add salmon; simmer, uncovered, for 3 minutes or until almost cooked, drain. Cool slightly; cut or break salmon into chunks.

4 Combine pasta, onion, capers, tomato, cucumber, rind and juice in a large bowl; season to taste. Add salmon and pesto; toss gently to combine.

rocket pesto Blend or process rocket, cheese, nuts and garlic until smooth. With motor operating, add oil in a thin, steady stream; blend until pesto thickens. Season to taste.

prep + cook time 35 minutes **serves** 6
nutritional count per serving 35.6g total fat
(6g saturated fat); 3089kJ (739 cal);
61.5g carbohydrate; 39.7g protein; 5.4g fibre

tip Use a medium heat to cook chicken so the sesame seeds don't burn before the chicken is cooked through.

sesame chicken and honey soy dressing

600g (1¼ pounds) chicken breast fillets, halved lengthways

1 egg white, beaten lightly

½ cup (75g) sesame seeds

2 tablespoons olive oil

100g (3 ounces) mixed baby asian greens

1 small red onion (100g), sliced thinly

⅔ cup (100g) coarsely chopped roasted unsalted cashews

honey soy dressing

¼ cup (60ml) lemon juice

2 tablespoons light soy sauce

1 tablespoon olive oil

2 teaspoons honey

½ teaspoon sesame oil

1 Dip chicken in egg white, then coat in sesame seeds.
2 Heat oil in a large frying pan over medium heat; cook chicken, in batches, for 5 minutes or until browned both sides and just cooked through. Cover chicken; stand for 5 minutes then slice thickly.
3 Meanwhile, make honey soy dressing.
4 Combine greens, onion and nuts in a medium bowl; divide between serving plates, top with chicken, drizzle with dressing.

honey soy dressing Combine ingredients in a small bowl.

prep + cook time 25 minutes serves 4
nutritional count per serving 45.9g total fat
(8g saturated fat); 2638kJ (631 cal);
11.8g carbohydrate; 42.1g protein; 3.8g fibre

grilled lamb and lebanese chickpea salad

3 cloves garlic, crushed

¼ cup (60ml) lemon juice

1 tablespoon olive oil

2 teaspoons ground cumin

750g (1½ pounds) lamb backstraps

2 tablespoons lemon juice, extra

2 tablespoons olive oil, extra

800g (1½ pounds) canned chickpeas (garbanzo beans), rinsed, drained

3 medium roma (egg) tomatoes (225g), cut into wedges

1 lebanese cucumber (130g), halved lengthways, sliced thinly

1 medium red onion (170g), sliced thinly

½ cup coarsely chopped fresh mint

½ cup coarsely chopped fresh flat-leaf parsley

1 Combine garlic, juice, oil, cumin and lamb in a large bowl; stand for 10 minutes.
2 Drain lamb; reserve marinade. Season lamb; cook on heated, oiled grill plate (or grill or barbecue) over medium-high heat for 10 minutes or until browned all over and cooked as desired, brushing occasionally with marinade. Cover to keep warm.
3 Whisk extra juice and extra oil in a large bowl; season to taste. Add remaining ingredients; toss gently to combine.
4 Thinly slice lamb; serve salad topped with lamb.

prep + cook time 30 minutes **serves** 4
nutritional count per serving 33.2g total fat
(9.8g saturated fat); 2537kJ (607 cal);
23.3g carbohydrate; 49.5g protein; 9.1g fibre

tips This recipe would also work well with chicken or fish. For a fuller flavour, marinate the lamb for 3 hours or overnight.

tips You can also use pancetta or bacon in this recipe. Try using a medley mix of tomatoes available from some supermarkets and greengrocers; halve the larger tomatoes and leave the smaller ones whole.

tomato, mozzarella and prosciutto salad

3 slices prosciutto (45g)

3 large roma (egg) tomatoes (270g), chopped coarsely

300g (9½ ounces) cherry bocconcini, chopped coarsely

1 medium avocado (250g), chopped coarsely

125g (4 ounces) mixed salad leaves

2 tablespoons olive oil

1 Cook prosciutto in a heated medium frying pan over medium heat until crisp; drain on kitchen paper. When cool enough to handle, break into pieces.
2 Combine prosciutto, tomato, cheese, avocado and salad leaves in a serving bowl. Drizzle with oil; season to taste.

prep + cook time 10 minutes **serves** 4
nutritional count per serving 31.2g total fat
(11.2g saturated fat); 1488kJ (356 cal);
1.8g carbohydrate; 16.9g protein; 2.1g fibre

five-spice pork and nashi in chilli plum dressing

600g (1¼ pounds) pork fillets, trimmed

2 teaspoons vegetable oil

1 teaspoon chinese five-spice powder

300g (9½ ounces) mizuna

2 green onions (scallions), sliced thinly

2 medium nashi (400g), sliced thinly

chilli plum dressing

¼ cup (60ml) plum sauce

1 tablespoon water

1 tablespoon lemon juice

1 fresh long red chilli, sliced thinly

1 Combine pork, oil and five-spice in a large bowl; stand for 10 minutes.
2 Cook pork on a heated oiled grill plate (or grill or barbecue) over medium heat for 20 minutes or until browned all over and just cooked through. Cover to keep warm.
3 Meanwhile, make chilli plum dressing.
4 Thickly slice pork. Combine mizuna, onion and nashi in a large bowl with two-thirds of the dressing. Serve salad topped with pork; drizzle with remaining dressing.

chilli plum dressing Combine ingredients in a screw-top jar; shake well.

prep + cook time 30 minutes **serves** 4
nutritional count per serving 14.8g total fat
(4.3g saturated fat); 1522kJ (364 cal);
22.5g carbohydrate; 33.3g protein; 3.1g fibre

tips You can use apples or firm pears instead of the nashi, if you prefer. Refrigerate the pork for 3 hours or overnight for a more intense flavour, if you like.

tips Dressing can be made 3 days ahead; keep refrigerated. Croûtons can be made several hours ahead; store in an airtight container at room temperature. For a quicker version, use bottled caesar dressing.

chicken caesar salad

4 slices white bread (180g)

2 tablespoons olive oil

4 rindless bacon slices (260g), sliced thinly

3 cups (480g) coarsely chopped barbecued chicken

1 large cos (romaine) lettuce, trimmed, torn coarsely

6 green onions (scallions), sliced thinly

1 cup (80g) flaked parmesan

caesar dressing

¾ cup (225g) whole-egg mayonnaise

1 tablespoon lemon juice

4 drained anchovy fillets, chopped finely

3 teaspoons dijon mustard

1 tablespoon water

1 Preheat oven to 160°C/325°F.

2 To make croûtons: discard crusts from bread, cut bread into 2cm (¾ inch) squares; toss with oil in a medium bowl. Place bread, in a single layer, on an oven tray; toast in oven for 10 minutes.

3 Cook bacon in a small frying pan over medium-high heat, stirring, until browned and crisp. Drain on kitchen paper.

4 Make caesar dressing.

5 Combine half the chicken, half the bacon, half the croûtons and half the dressing in a large bowl with lettuce, half the onion and half the cheese; toss gently.

6 Divide salad between serving plates. Top with remaining chicken, bacon, croûtons, onion and cheese; drizzle with remaining dressing.

caesar dressing Blend ingredients until mixture is smooth.

prep + cook time 35 minutes **serves** 4
nutritional count per serving 53.5g total fat (13.8g saturated fat); 3595kJ (860 cal); 34.9g carbohydrate; 57.6g protein; 5.6g fibre

CLASSIC SALADS

greek salad

Whisk ¼ cup olive oil, 1 tablespoon lemon juice, 1 tablespoon white wine vinegar, 1 tablespoon finely chopped fresh oregano and 1 crushed garlic clove in a large bowl. Cut 3 medium tomatoes into wedges; coarsely chop 2 lebanese cucumbers. Thinly slice 1 small red onion and 1 small red capsicum (bell pepper). Add tomato, cucumber, onion and capsicum to bowl with ½ cup pitted black olives and 200g (6½oz) coarsely chopped fetta; mix gently to combine.

prep time 20 minutes **serves** 4
nutritional count per serving 25.8g total fat (9.6g saturated fat); 1359kJ (325 cal); 10.8g carbohydrate; 11.5g protein; 3.2g fibre

tomato and herb salad

Halve 900g (1¾lb) baby heirloom tomatoes. Place tomato, 2 tablespoons coarsely chopped fresh mint, ¼ cup coarsely chopped fresh flat-leaf parsley and 2 tablespoons finely chopped fresh dill in a medium bowl. Place 2 cloves crushed garlic, 2 tablespoons lemon juice, 1 tablespoon olive oil and 2 teaspoons white vinegar in a screw-top jar; shake well. Drizzle dressing over salad; toss gently to combine.

prep time 10 minutes **serves** 4
nutritional count per serving 4.9g total fat (0.7g saturated fat); 362kJ (87 cal); 5.7g carbohydrate; 2.6g protein; 3.5g fibre

waldorf salad

Combine ¾ cup mayonnaise and ¼ cup lemon juice in a large
bowl. Add 5 thickly sliced trimmed celery stalks, 2 thinly sliced
small red apples, 1 thinly sliced small red onion, 1 cup toasted
walnuts and 1 cup loosely packed fresh flat-leaf parsley leaves;
toss gently to combine.

prep time 20 minutes **serves** 4
nutritional count per serving 35.7g total fat (3.1g saturated fat);
1852kJ (443 cal); 22.4g carbohydrate; 5.8g protein; 6.3g fibre

mixed cabbage coleslaw

Whisk ⅓ cup olive oil, 2 tablespoons apple cider vinegar and
2 teaspoons dijon mustard in a large bowl. Mix in 2 cups finely
shredded green cabbage, 2 cups finely shredded red cabbage,
2 cups finely shredded wombok (napa cabbage), 1 coarsely
grated medium carrot and 4 thinly sliced green onions (scallions);
toss gently to combine.

prep time 20 minutes **serves** 4
nutritional count per serving 18.4g total fat (2.6g saturated fat);
836kJ (200 cal); 4.5g carbohydrate; 2.4g protein; 4.7g fibre

tip Any leftover salad mixture without dressing can be added to chilli con carne, beef casserole or a basic bolognese sauce.

mexican beef salad

35g (1 ounce) packet taco spice mix

600g (1¼-pound) piece beef rump steak

420g (13 ounces) canned four-bean mix, rinsed, drained

125g (4 ounces) canned corn kernels, rinsed, drained

2 large tomatoes (440g), chopped finely

½ cup coarsely chopped fresh coriander (cilantro)

lime wedges, to serve

1 Rub spice mix over both sides of steak. Heat a large frying pan over medium-high heat. Cook steak for 8 minutes or until browned and cooked as desired. Remove from pan; cover to keep warm.

2 Combine beans, corn, tomato and coriander in a medium bowl; season to taste.

3 Slice steak thickly. Divide salad between serving plates; top with steak. Serve with lime wedges.

prep + cook time 15 minutes **serves** 4
nutritional count per serving 10.7g total fat
(4.6g saturated fat); 1392kJ (333 cal);
15.9g carbohydrate; 39.8g protein; 6.6g fibre

serving suggestion Guacamole.

warm lamb and pasta provençale salad

375g (12 ounces) rigatoni pasta

600g (1¼ pounds) lamb fillets

¾ cup (115g) pitted black olives, halved

1 cup (150g) drained semi-dried tomatoes in oil, chopped coarsely

400g (12½ ounces) canned artichoke hearts, rinsed, drained, halved

1 small red onion (100g), sliced thinly

60g (2 ounces) baby rocket (arugula)

½ cup (120g) green olive tapenade

2 tablespoons olive oil

2 tablespoons lemon juice

1 Cook pasta in a large saucepan of boiling water until just tender; drain.

2 Meanwhile, season lamb; cook lamb in a heated oiled large frying pan over medium-high heat for 6 minutes or until browned all over and cooked as desired. Cover lamb; stand for 5 minutes then slice thickly.

3 Combine pasta with lamb, olives, tomato, artichokes, onion and rocket in a large bowl. Combine tapenade, oil and juice in a small bowl; season to taste. Add tapenade mixture to pasta mixture; toss gently.

prep + cook time 30 minutes **serves** 6
nutritional count per serving 16.9g total fat
(3.4g saturated fat); 2203kJ (527 cal);
57.4g carbohydrate; 32g protein; 7.5g fibre

tips You can use any short pasta; penne, curls, fusilli, farfalle and macaroni will all work well. For an even faster option, use the shredded meat from a barbecued chicken or 12 slices of chopped salami.

thai beef salad

¼ cup (60ml) fish sauce

¼ cup (60ml) lime juice

500g (1 pound) beef rump steak

1 tablespoon grated palm sugar

2 teaspoons soy sauce

1 clove garlic, crushed

3 lebanese cucumbers (390g), seeded, sliced thinly

4 fresh small red thai (serrano) chillies, sliced thinly

4 green onions (scallions), sliced thinly

250g (8 ounces) cherry tomatoes, halved

¼ cup firmly packed fresh vietnamese mint leaves

½ cup firmly packed fresh coriander leaves (cilantro)

½ cup firmly packed fresh thai basil leaves

1 Combine 2 tablespoons of the fish sauce and 1 tablespoon of the juice in a medium bowl with beef. Cover; stand for 10 minutes.

2 Drain beef; reserve marinade. Cook beef on a heated oiled grill plate (or grill or barbecue) until cooked as desired, brushing occasionally with marinade. Cover beef; rest for 5 minutes, then slice beef thinly.

3 Meanwhile, place sugar, soy sauce, garlic, remaining fish sauce and remaining juice in a screw-top jar; shake well.

4 Combine cucumber, chilli, onion, tomato and herbs in a large bowl. Add beef and dressing; toss gently to combine.

prep + cook time 35 minutes **serves** 4

nutritional count per serving 8.7g total fat (3.8g saturated fat); 986kJ (236 cal); 8.2g carbohydrate; 30.6g protein; 3.4g fibre

tip For a more intense flavour, marinate the beef for 3 hours or overnight.

tip We used a mild harissa available in jars from delis and gourmet food stores. If using traditional harissa in a tube, you will need only a teaspoon, or less, as it is extremely hot.

fattoush with harissa-rubbed lamb

600g (1¼ pounds) lamb backstraps

¼ cup (75g) mild harissa sauce

¼ cup (60ml) olive oil

3 pocket pitta breads (255g)

3 medium tomatoes (450g), cut into wedges

1 large green capsicum (350g), sliced thickly

2 lebanese cucumbers (260g), halved, sliced thinly

½ cup coarsely chopped fresh mint

1 cup firmly packed fresh flat-leaf parsley leaves

¼ cup (60ml) lemon juice

1 clove garlic, crushed

1 Combine lamb and harissa in a medium bowl; rub harissa into lamb, stand for 10 minutes.

2 Heat 1 tablespoon of the oil in a large frying pan over medium heat; cook lamb for 10 minutes or until browned all over and cooked as desired. Cover to keep warm.

3 Meanwhile, preheat grill (broiler). Split pittas in half; grill both sides until browned lightly.

4 Combine remaining ingredients in a large bowl; season to taste. Break pitta into pieces over salad. Thickly slice lamb; serve fattoush topped with lamb.

prep + cook time 30 minutes **serves** 4
nutritional count per serving 28.9g total fat
(8.2g saturated fat); 2416kJ (578 cal);
36.7g carbohydrate; 39.6g protein; 6.4g fibre

tip For a more intense flavour, marinate the lamb for 1 hour.

tandoori chicken, spinach and mint with spiced yoghurt

⅓ cup (100g) tandoori paste

¼ cup (70g) plain yoghurt

800g (1½ pounds) chicken tenderloins

1 tablespoon vegetable oil

8 large uncooked pappadums

150g (4½ ounces) baby spinach leaves

2 lebanese cucumbers (260g), sliced thickly

250g (8 ounces) cherry tomatoes, halved

1 cup firmly packed fresh mint leaves

spiced yoghurt

1 clove garlic, crushed

¾ cup (210g) plain yoghurt

1 tablespoon lemon juice

1 teaspoon each ground cumin and coriander

1 Combine paste and yoghurt in a medium bowl with chicken.
2 Make spiced yoghurt.
3 Heat oil in a large frying pan over medium heat. Season chicken; cook, in batches, for 5 minutes or until browned all over and just cooked through.
4 Meanwhile, microwave 2 pappadums at a time on HIGH (100%) for 30 seconds.
5 Combine chicken in a large bowl with spinach, cucumber, tomato and mint. Drizzle with yoghurt; serve with pappadums.

spiced yoghurt Combine ingredients in a small jug; season to taste.

prep + cook time 35 minutes **serves** 4
nutritional count per serving 12.5g total fat
(3.4g saturated fat); 1731kJ (414 cal);
16.4g carbohydrate; 55.1g protein; 6.7g fibre

tips For a more intense flavour, marinate the chicken for 3 hours or overnight. Any leftover chicken, salad and yoghurt can be refrigerated separately then served in a wrap or tortilla the next day. We used large plain pappadums here, but there are many sizes and flavour combinations to choose from.

tip The recipe can be prepared several hours ahead; however, roast the beef close to serving.

oven-roasted beef fillet and beetroot with horseradish crème fraîche

500g (1 pound) piece beef eye fillet, trimmed

2 tablespoons wholegrain (seeded) mustard

1 tablespoon horseradish cream

2 tablespoons olive oil

1kg (2 pounds) fresh baby beetroot (beets), trimmed

150g (4½ ounces) baby rocket (arugula)

2 lebanese cucumbers (260g), sliced thinly

1 cup loosely packed fresh flat-leaf parsley

parmesan croûtons

1 small french bread stick (150g)

1 tablespoon olive oil

½ cup (40g) finely grated parmesan

horseradish crème fraîche

¼ cup (60g) crème fraîche

2 tablespoons horseradish cream

1 tablespoon lemon juice

1 Preheat oven to 220°C/425°F.

2 Tie beef with kitchen string at 3cm (1¼-inch) intervals. Combine mustard, horseradish and oil in a small jug; brush beef all over with mixture. Season.

3 Place beef in a medium oiled baking dish with beetroot; roast, uncovered, for 10 minutes.

4 Reduce oven temperature to 200°C/400°F; roast for a further 15 minutes or until beef is cooked as desired and beetroot is tender. Cover beef; rest for 10 minutes then slice thinly. Peel and halve beetroots.

5 Meanwhile, make parmesan croûtons and horseradish crème fraîche.

6 Combine rocket, cucumber, parsley and beetroot in a large bowl; season to taste. Serve salad topped with croûtons and beef; drizzle with crème fraîche.

parmesan croûtons Slice bread thinly; place on an oven tray. Brush slices with oil. Bake in oven, towards the end of the beef cooking time, for 5 minutes or until bread browns lightly. Sprinkle with cheese, return to oven until cheese melts.

horseradish crème fraîche Combine ingredients in a small bowl.

prep + cook time 40 minutes **serves** 4
nutritional count per serving 33.8g total fat
(12.2g saturated fat); 2704kJ (647 cal);
40.7g carbohydrate; 40.2g protein; 10.5g fibre

tips You can poach, shred and refrigerate the chicken a day ahead, and you can also prepare the dressing and salad vegetables a day ahead. Keep them refrigerated, then simply combine with the noodles when you're ready. Or, poach and shred the chicken, and use it warm with the salad ingredients and noodles.

chicken and vermicelli noodle salad

2 litres (8 cups) water

800g (1½ pounds) chicken breast fillets

200g (6½ ounces) rice vermicelli

150g (4½ ounces) snow peas

8 green onions (scallions)

2 medium carrots (240g)

½ medium wombok (napa cabbage) (500g), shredded finely

2 cups (160g) bean sprouts

1 cup firmly packed fresh mint leaves

1 cup firmly packed fresh coriander leaves (cilantro)

½ cup (70g) roasted unsalted peanuts, chopped coarsely

sweet chilli dressing

½ cup (125ml) lime juice

2 tablespoons fish sauce

3 teaspoons sambal oelek

2 teaspoons sesame oil

1 tablespoon brown sugar

1 clove garlic, crushed

1 Bring the water to the boil in a large saucepan; add chicken. Simmer, uncovered, for 10 minutes or until chicken is cooked. Cool chicken in poaching liquid for 10 minutes; drain. Using two forks, shred chicken coarsely.
2 Place vermicelli in a large heatproof bowl, cover with boiling water; stand until tender, drain. Rinse under cold water, drain.
3 Meanwhile, make sweet chilli dressing.
4 Slice snow peas and onions diagonally into thin strips. Halve carrots crossways; cut into matchsticks. Combine peas, onion, carrot, wombok, sprouts, herbs and chicken in a large bowl with vermicelli; drizzle with dressing. Serve salad sprinkled with nuts.

sweet chilli dressing Combine ingredients in a screw-top jar; shake well.

prep + cook time 40 minutes serves 6
nutritional count per serving 15.1g total fat (3.1g saturated fat); 1772kJ (424 cal); 30.9g carbohydrate; 37.7g protein; 6.4g fibre

desserts

Saving the best until last, desserts are always a crowd-pleaser. These effortless recipes are sure to meet with approval.

tips Frangipane is a delicious almond-flavoured filling for pies and tarts. We've used mixed berries in this recipe, but use any berries you like. The berries should be frozen so the colour won't bleed dramatically through the frangipane as it cooks.

berry frangipane tart

1 sheet puff pastry

300g (9½ ounces) frozen mixed berries

frangipane

80g (2½ ounces) butter, softened

½ teaspoon vanilla extract

⅓ cup (75g) caster (superfine) sugar

2 egg yolks

1 tablespoon plain (all-purpose) flour

1 cup (120g) ground almonds

1 Preheat oven to 220°C/425°F. Grease a 20cm x 30cm (8 inch x 12 inch) rectangular slice pan.

2 Roll pastry until large enough to cover base and sides of pan; line pan with pastry, press into sides. Prick pastry all over with a fork; freeze for 5 minutes.

3 Place another pan on top of pastry; bake 5 minutes. Remove top pan; bake 5 minutes or until pastry is browned lightly. Cool for 5 minutes. Reduce oven temperature to 180°C/350°F.

4 Meanwhile, make frangipane.

5 Spread frangipane over pastry base. Sprinkle with frozen berries, press into frangipane. Bake for 25 minutes or until browned lightly.

frangipane Beat butter, extract, sugar and egg yolks in a small bowl with an electric mixer until light and fluffy. Stir in flour and nuts.

prep + cook time 40 minutes **serves** 6
nutritional count per serving 30.2g total fat (11.9g saturated fat); 1722kJ (412 cal); 26.4g carbohydrate; 7.7g protein; 3.3g fibre

serving suggestion Custard, ice-cream or thick cream.

poached pears with chocolate sauce

1.5 litres (6 cups) water

2 cups (500ml) port

½ cup (110g) caster (superfine) sugar

2 x 8cm (3¼ inch) strips orange rind

2 tablespoons orange juice

8 corella pears (480g), peeled

¼ cup (60ml) pouring cream

75g (2½ ounces) milk chocolate, chopped coarsely

1 Combine the water, port, sugar, rind and juice in a large saucepan. Add pears; bring to the boil. Reduce heat; simmer, covered, for 15 minutes or until pears are tender. Cool pears in syrup (or pears can be served warm).

2 Remove pears from syrup with a slotted spoon; strain syrup into a medium heatproof bowl. Return 2 cups of the strained syrup to the pan (discard the remaining syrup); bring to the boil. Boil, uncovered, for 15 minutes or until syrup is reduced to about ½ cup; stir in cream, simmer until slightly thickened. Add chocolate, stir until smooth. Serve pears drizzled with chocolate sauce.

prep + cook time 40 minutes **serves** 4
nutritional count per serving 11.7g total fat
(7.4g saturated fat); 2182kJ (522 cal);
69.4g carbohydrate; 2.4g protein; 1.9g fibre

serving suggestion Ice-cream

tips If you can't find corella pears, use four beurre bosc pears instead. The same quantity of red wine can be used in place of the port; the end result may not be as sweet, so adjust sweetening accordingly. Pears can be reheated gently in the syrup, or served cold. You can sprinkle some fine strips of orange rind over the pears to serve.

tips   Mini pavlova shells are available from most supermarkets. You will need around six passionfruit for this recipe.

passionfruit and banana crush

300ml thickened (heavy) cream

2 tablespoons lemon-flavoured spread

50g (1½ ounces) mini pavlova shells, chopped coarsely

4 small bananas (520g), chopped coarsely

½ cup (125ml) passionfruit pulp

1 Beat cream and spread in a small bowl with an electric mixer until soft peaks form.

2 Layer lemon cream, pavlova pieces, banana and passionfruit into four serving glasses.

prep time 15 minutes **serves** 4
nutritional count per serving 28.6g total fat (18.5g saturated fat); 1839kJ (440 cal); 38.9g carbohydrate; 4.4g protein; 6.3g fibre

freeform tiramisu

½ cup (125ml) strong espresso coffee, cooled

½ cup (125ml) coffee-flavoured liqueur

10 sponge finger biscuits (savoiardi), halved crossways

⅔ cup (160ml) thickened (heavy) cream

¼ cup (40g) icing (confectioners') sugar

250g (8 ounces) mascarpone cheese

cocoa, for dusting

1 Combine coffee and ⅓ cup of the liqueur in a small bowl. Dip biscuits, one at a time, into coffee mixture. Line four 1 cup (250ml) serving glasses with biscuits; drizzle with any remaining coffee mixture.

2 Beat cream and sifted icing sugar in a small bowl with an electric mixer until soft peaks form; beat in mascarpone and remaining liqueur. Divide mixture between glasses; dust with sifted cocoa, if you like.

prep time 10 minutes **serves** 4
nutritional count per serving 37g total fat
(23.5g saturated fat); 2550kJ (610 cal);
47.4g carbohydrate; 8.6g protein; 0.4g fibre

tips   To make a strong espresso coffee, combine 2 tablespoons instant espresso coffee and ½ cup boiling water. This recipe is best made close to serving.

tips This English dessert is often called Eton Mess, taking its name from Eton College, one of Britain's most famous public schools, where it was traditionally served. The 'mess' part is because it was all mixed together in one big bowl.

strawberry crush

500g (1 pound) strawberries, hulled, quartered

1 tablespoon orange-flavoured liqueur

2 tablespoons icing (confectioners') sugar

300ml thickened (heavy) cream, whipped

¾ cup (200g) thick greek-style yoghurt

5 pavlova nests (50g), crumbled coarsely

1 Combine strawberries, liqueur and sifted icing sugar in a medium bowl. Stand 5 minutes; stir well.
2 Meanwhile, combine cream, yoghurt and pavlova nests in a medium bowl.
3 Place half the cream mixture in four 1-cup (250ml) serving glasses. Top with half the strawberry mixture, then remaining cream mixture and strawberry mixture. Serve immediately.

prep time 15 minutes **serves** 4
nutritional count per serving 29.9g total fat (19.5g saturated fat); 1747kJ (418 cal); 27.2g carbohydrate; 6.4g protein; 2.8g fibre

tip Pastry pieces can be made a day ahead; store in an airtight container at room temperature. We've used mixed berries in this recipe, however, you can use any berries you like.

mascarpone berry matchsticks

300g (10 ounces) frozen mixed berries

2 tablespoons citrus-flavoured liqueur

⅓ cup (55g) icing (confectioners') sugar

1 sheet butter puff pastry

200g (6½ ounces) mascarpone cheese

½ cup (125ml) thickened (heavy) cream

1 Preheat oven to 220°C/425°F. Line an oven tray with baking paper.

2 Place berries in a medium bowl; sprinkle with liqueur and 1 tablespoon of the sifted icing sugar. Stand until thawed, stirring occasionally.

3 Cut pastry sheet into 8 rectangles. Place rectangles on an oven tray; dust with 2 teaspoons of the sifted icing sugar. Bake 10 minutes or until puffed and browned. Cool.

4 Beat mascarpone, cream and 2 tablespoons of the remaining sifted icing sugar in a small bowl with an electric mixer until soft peaks form.

5 Sandwich mascarpone mixture, berries and any berry juices between pastry pieces. Dust matchsticks with remaining sifted icing sugar.

prep + cook time 35 minutes **serves** 4
nutritional count per serving 37.8g total fat (23.3g saturated fat); 2391kJ (572 cal); 42.8g carbohydrate; 8g protein; 3.5g fibre

SUNDAES

chocolate sundaes

To make the hot chocolate sauce, stir 200g (6½oz) coarsely chopped dark (semi sweet) chocolate and ½ cup thickened cream in a small saucepan over low heat until chocolate is melted and sauce is smooth – do not overheat. Place a little of the hot chocolate sauce in the bottom of six ¾-cup (180ml) serving glasses; divide 2 litres (8 cups) vanilla ice-cream, 100g (3oz) marshmallows, more chocolate sauce, ½ cup crushed nuts and 6 ice-cream wafers between glasses.

prep + cook time 10 minutes **serves** 6
nutritional count per serving 44.3g total fat
(27.4g saturated fat); 3204kJ (765 cal);
81.2g carbohydrate; 13.7g protein; 0.4g fibre

banana split with caramel sauce

Stir ⅔ cup thickened cream, 60g (2oz) butter and ¾ cup firmly packed brown sugar in a small saucepan, over medium heat, until smooth. Reduce heat, simmer, uncovered, for 2 minutes. Cool 10 minutes. Meanwhile, beat an extra 1 cup thickened cream in a small bowl with an electric mixer until soft peaks form. Divide half the sauce among four serving dishes; top with 2 thinly sliced large bananas, 2 cups (500ml) vanilla ice-cream, remaining sauce and extra whipped cream; sprinkle over ½ cup toasted flaked almonds.

prep + cook time 20 minutes **serves** 4
nutritional count per serving 69.3g total fat
(41.9g saturated fat); 3971kJ (949 cal);
76.3g carbohydrate; 9.7g protein; 0.9g fibre

warm caramel sundaes

Stir 125g (4oz) chopped butter, 300ml thickened cream and 1 cup firmly packed brown sugar in a medium saucepan over low heat until butter is melted. Blend 1 tablespoon cornflour and 1 tablespoon water; stir into pan, bring to the boil. Reduce heat; simmer, uncovered, for 3 minutes or until thickened slightly. Divide 2 cups (500ml) vanilla ice-cream among four serving bowls, top with warm caramel sauce and 100g (3oz) coarsely chopped jersey caramels.

prep + cook time 20 minutes **serves** 4
nutritional count per serving 67.8g total fat
(44.1g saturated fat); 4304kJ (1028 cal);
103g carbohydrate; 7.1g protein; 0g fibre

summer berry sundaes

Stir ¼ cup caster (superfine) sugar and 500g (1lb) mixed frozen berries in a medium saucepan over medium heat, without boiling, until sugar dissolves; bring to the boil. Reduce heat, simmer, uncovered, for 5 minutes or until berries soften. Stir in 1 tablespoon orange-flavoured liqueur; cool for 10 minutes. Layer 4 cups vanilla ice-cream, berry mixture and ⅔ cup coarsely chopped roasted macadamias among four serving glasses.

prep + cook time 20 minutes **serves** 4
nutritional count per serving 33.4g total fat
(13.9g saturated fat); 2328kJ (556 cal);
58.3g carbohydrate; 8.5g protein; 1.3g fibre

berry hazelnut cups

250g (8 ounces) raspberries

2 tablespoons icing (confectioners') sugar

300ml thickened (heavy) cream

2 tablespoons hazelnut-flavoured liqueur

90g (3-ounce) packet brandy baskets

⅓ cup (45g) coarsely chopped roasted hazelnuts

1 Blend or process half the raspberries and half the icing sugar until smooth; strain through a fine sieve into a small jug.
2 Beat cream, remaining icing sugar and liqueur in a small bowl with an electric mixer until soft peaks form.
3 Divide cream mixture into brandy baskets; top with remaining raspberries and nuts. Drizzle with raspberry sauce.

prep time 15 minutes **serves** 6
nutritional count per serving 40.4g total fat
(23.5g saturated fat); 2174kJ (520 cal);
26.9g carbohydrate; 4.7g protein; 5.4g fibre

tips You need 6 brandy baskets for this recipe. They are available from most supermarkets and delis.
Roasted skinned hazelnuts are available in supermarkets. If you can't find them, spread whole hazelnuts on an oven tray. Roast at 180°C/350°F for 8 minutes or until browned lightly and skin is beginning to split. Tip nuts into a clean tea towel; rub vigorously to remove skins. Cool slightly then chop coarsely.

tip Serving the tarte tartin on warmed plates keeps the caramel soft.

banana tarte tatin

1 cup (220g) caster (superfine) sugar

2 tablespoons water

125g (4 ounces) cold unsalted butter, chopped

1 sheet butter puff pastry

4 large bananas (520g), peeled, cut into 2cm (¾ inch) pieces

2 tablespoons caster (superfine) sugar, extra

1 To make caramel sauce, combine sugar with the water in a medium saucepan; stir over heat, without boiling, until sugar is dissolved. Bring to the boil; boil, uncovered, without stirring, for 10 minutes or until it turns a caramel colour, remove from heat. Using a metal whisk, gradually whisk butter into caramel until combined. Pour sauce into 20cm (8 inch) ovenproof frying pan. Cool slightly.

2 Meanwhile, preheat oven to 220°C/425°F.

3 Cut a 23cm (9 inch) circle from pastry.

4 Place banana, cut-side up, on top of caramel; top with pastry, making sure the pastry sits evenly over the banana. Press the overhanging pastry down the sides of the pan, tightly against the banana, to form an edge. Sprinkle pastry with extra sugar.

5 Bake, uncovered, for 15 minutes or until pastry is browned and cooked through. Invert tarte tatin onto a warmed large plate to serve.

prep + cook time 35 minutes **serves** 4
nutritional count per serving 35.6g total fat (17.8g saturated fat); 2989kJ (715 cal); 93.5g carbohydrate; 4g protein; 2.5g fibre

serving suggestion Ice-cream or cream.

tips Decorate the trifle with chocolate shavings, if you like. Just run a sharp vegetable peeler down the side of a slightly softened block of chocolate. The harder you press the thicker the shavings will be. We used a small block of dark eating chocolate. The syrup can be made several hours ahead.

chocolate trifle with blueberries and cream

¼ cup (55g) firmly packed brown sugar

½ cup (125ml) sherry

2 cinnamon sticks

500g (1 pound) store-bought chocolate cake

300ml thickened (heavy) cream, whipped

150g (5 ounces) fresh blueberries

1 Combine sugar, sherry and cinnamon in a small saucepan; bring to the boil then simmer, uncovered, until sugar is dissolved. Cool syrup.
2 Discard any icing from cake; cut cake into 2cm (¾ inch) cubes. Divide cake between four 1½-cup (375ml) serving glasses; drizzle with syrup. Top with cream and blueberries.

prep + cook time 25 minutes (+ cooling) **serves** 4
nutritional count per serving 51.2g total fat
(32.9g saturated fat); 3557kJ (851 cal);
78.8g carbohydrate; 10.6g protein; 2.6g fibre

apple and raspberry crumbles

4 medium green apples (600g), peeled, chopped coarsely

2 teaspoons finely grated lemon rind

¼ cup (60ml) lemon juice

¼ cup (55g) firmly packed brown sugar

2 teaspoons mixed spice

2 tablespoons water

500g (1 pound) frozen raspberries

125g (4 ounces) scotch finger biscuits, crumbled

1 Preheat oven to 220°C/425°F.

2 Cook apples, rind, juice and sugar in a large frying pan until apples begin to caramelise. Stir in spice, the water and raspberries.

3 Divide mixture into four 1-cup (250ml) shallow ovenproof dishes; top with biscuit crumbs. Place dishes on an oven tray.

4 Bake 10 minutes or until crumbles are heated through.

prep + cook time 30 minutes **serves** 4

nutritional count per serving 8.4g total fat (4.1g saturated fat); 1346kJ (322 cal); 53g carbohydrate; 3.9g protein; 9.5g fibre

serving suggestion Dust with sifted icing sugar; serve with ice-cream or double cream.

tips We used granny smith apples in this recipe. You need 2 lemons for the rind and juice.

tips You need to make this recipe in the morning, or start it the night before, to allow it time to freeze. To un-mould the ice-blocks, remove them from the freezer and stand for 5 minutes. Wrap each ice-block in a hot damp tea towel until ice-block becomes loose.

coconut berry ice-blocks

300g (9½ ounces) frozen raspberries

½ cup (110g) caster (superfine) sugar

2 cups (500ml) thickened (heavy) cream

2 cups (500ml) coconut cream

16 ice-block sticks

1 Stir raspberries and sugar in a medium saucepan over medium-high heat until sugar dissolves; bring to the boil. Reduce heat; simmer, uncovered, for 5 minutes or until mixture thickens slightly. Transfer to a small bowl; refrigerate until cold.
2 Meanwhile, beat thickened cream in a small bowl with an electric mixer until firm peaks form; add coconut cream, beat only until combined. Transfer mixture to a large bowl.
3 Gentle fold raspberry mixture through cream mixture to get a rippled effect. Spoon mixture into ⅓-cup (80ml) ice-block moulds; insert stick. Freeze for about 4 hours or until set.
4 Remove ice-blocks from freezer; stand for 5 minutes before removing from moulds.

prep + cook time 20 minutes (+ freezing) **makes** 16
nutritional count per ice-block 17.7g total fat (13g saturated fat); 846kJ (202 cal); 10.1g carbohydrate; 1.4g protein; 1.3g fibre

tip We used Malibu in this recipe, but you can use any coconut-flavoured liqueur you prefer.

banana and coconut cream parfait

¾ cup (180ml) thickened cream

2 tablespoons icing sugar

2 tablespoons Malibu

300ml mango coconut crème ice-cream

4 large bananas (920g), sliced thinly

½ cup (25g) flaked coconut, toasted

1 Beat cream, icing sugar and liqueur in a small bowl with an electric mixer until soft peaks form.
2 Layer ice-cream, banana, coconut and cream mixture in four 1½-cup (375ml) serving glasses.

prep time 15 minutes **serves** 4
nutritional count per serving 30.7g total fat (20.8g saturated fat); 2197kJ (525 cal); 53.3g carbohydrate; 6.6g protein; 4.5g fibre

fruit and marshmallow dessert pizzas

8 x 11cm (4½-inch) round pizza bases (340g)

cooking-oil spray

1 small banana (130g), sliced thinly

250g (8 ounces) strawberries, quartered

60g (2 ounces) pink and white marshmallows

⅓ cup (80ml) caramel topping

1 Preheat oven to 240°C/475°F. Oil two oven or pizza trays; place in heated oven to heat up.
2 Place pizza bases on trays; spray with cooking oil.
3 Bake pizzas for 7 minutes; remove from oven. Top with banana, berries and marshmallows. Bake for 4 minutes or until bases are browned and crisp. Drizzle with caramel topping.

prep + cook time 15 minutes **makes** 8
nutritional count per pizza 1.8g total fat (0.3g saturated fat); 836kJ (200 cal); 41g carbohydrate; 5.1g protein; 2.5g fibre

tip Pizza bases are pre-packaged for home-made pizzas. The smaller-sized bases come plain (without sauce), which is what we've used here. You can use a larger plain base, if you like, just use an 11cm round cutter to cut the bases out of the dough.

glossary

artichoke hearts tender centre of the globe artichoke; purchased, in brine, canned or in glass jars.

bamboo shoots the tender shoots of bamboo plants, available in cans; must be rinsed and drained before use.

basil an aromatic herb; there are many types, but the most commonly used is sweet, or common, basil.

thai basil, also known as horapa, has a sweet licorice flavour; it is available from Asian grocery stores and most major supermarkets.

beans
butter also known as lima beans; large, flat, kidney-shaped bean, off-white in colour, with a mealy texture and mild taste.

cannellini a small white bean similar in appearance and flavour to other white beans (great northern, navy or haricot), all of which can be substituted for the other. Available dried or canned.

snake long (about 40cm/16 inches), thin, round, fresh green beans, Asian in origin, with a taste similar to green or french beans. Are also known as yard-long beans because of their (pre-metric) length.

sprouts also known as bean shoots; tender new growths of assorted beans and seeds germinated for consumption.

white see cannellini beans.

breadcrumbs
packaged fine-textured, crunchy, purchased white breadcrumbs.

panko also known as japanese breadcrumbs. They are available in two types: larger pieces and fine crumbs. Both have a lighter texture than Western-style breadcrumbs. They are at all Asian grocery stores and, unless you make rather coarse breadcrumbs from white bread that's either quite stale or gently toasted, nothing is an adequate substitute. Has a crunchy texture with a delicate, pale golden colour.

stale one- or two-day-old bread made into crumbs by blending or processing.

buk choy also known as bok choy, pak choi, chinese white cabbage or chinese chard; has a fresh, mild mustard taste. Use both stems and leaves. Baby buk choy, also known as pak kat farang or shanghai bok choy, is smaller and more tender than buk choy.

butter use salted or unsalted (sweet) butter; 125g is equal to one stick of butter (4 ounces).

capers grey-green buds of a warm climate shrub (usually Mediterranean); sold either dried and salted or pickled in a vinegar brine. Baby capers are very small and have a fuller flavour. Rinse well before using.

cheese
blue mould-treated cheeses mottled with blue veining. Varieties include firm and crumbly stilton types to mild, creamy brie-like cheeses.

cream known as philadelphia or philly; a soft, cows'-milk cheese sold at supermarkets. Also available as a spreadable light cream cheese – a blend of cottage and cream cheeses.

fetta, danish (also danish white fetta) this type of fetta is a smooth and creamy variation of the more traditional fetta cheeses. The cheese is popular for its ability to be cubed and sliced without crumbling, and tossed into salads. Danish fetta has a very different taste to traditional fetta cheese. It has a milder taste, which makes it popular as an ingredient in baking.

fetta, persian a soft, creamy fetta marinated in a blend of olive oil, garlic, herbs and spices. It is available from most larger supermarkets.

goat's made from goat's milk, has an earthy, strong taste; available in both soft and firm textures, in various shapes and sizes, and sometimes rolled in ash or herbs.

gorgonzola a creamy blue cheese having a mild, sweet taste.

gruyère a Swiss cheese with small holes and a nutty, slightly salty flavour.

haloumi a firm, cream-coloured sheep-milk cheese matured in brine; haloumi can be grilled or fried, briefly, without breaking down. Should be eaten while still warm as it becomes tough and rubbery on cooling.

mascarpone a cultured cream product made in much the same way as yoghurt. Is whitish to creamy yellow in colour, with a soft, creamy texture and a rich, sweet, slightly acidic, taste.

pizza a blend of grated mozzarella, cheddar and parmesan cheeses.

chilli generally, the smaller the chilli, the hotter it is. Use rubber gloves when seeding and chopping fresh chillies as they can burn your skin. Removing seeds and membranes lessens the heat level.

cayenne pepper a long, thin-fleshed, extremely hot red chilli usually sold dried and ground.

long available both fresh and dried; a generic term used for any moderately hot, long (6cm-8cm), thin chilli.

red thai a small, hot, bright red chilli.

chinese barbecued pork also called char siew. Has a sweet-sticky coating made from soy sauce, sherry, five-spice powder and hoisin sauce. Available from Asian food stores.

chinese cooking wine also known as shao hsing or chinese rice wine; made from fermented rice, wheat, sugar and salt with a 13.5 per cent alcohol content. Inexpensive and found in Asian food shops; if you can't find it, replace it with mirin or sherry.

chorizo a sausage of Spanish origin; made of coarsely ground pork and highly seasoned with garlic and chilli. They are deeply smoked, very spicy, and are available dry-cured or raw (which needs cooking).

coriander also known as pak chee, cilantro or chinese parsley; a bright-green leafy herb with a pungent flavour. Both the stems and roots of coriander are also used in cooking; wash well before using. Also available ground or as seeds; these should not be substituted for fresh coriander as the tastes are completely different.

cos lettuce also known as romaine.

couscous a fine, grain-like cereal product made from semolina.

cream we use fresh cream, also known as pure cream and pouring cream, unless otherwise stated.

cumin also known as zeera or comino; has a spicy, nutty flavour.

curry
curry powder a blend of ground spices used for convenience. Choose mild or hot to suit your taste.

green paste the hottest of the traditional pastes; contains chilli, garlic, onion, salt, lemon grass, spices and galangal.

tandoori paste a highly-seasoned classic East-Indian marinade flavoured with garlic, tamarind, ginger, coriander, chilli and other spices, and used to give foods the authentic red-orange tint of tandoor oven cooking.

tikka paste a medium-mild paste of chilli, coriander, cumin, lentil flour, garlic, ginger, turmeric, fennel, cloves, cinnamon and cardamom.

tom yum paste a Thai-style paste with a hot, spicy and sour flavour. Containing lemon grass, red chilli, sugar, onion, anchovy, galangal, kaffir lime and paprika. It is used to make the traditional spicy sour prawn soup known as tom yum goong.

dukkah is an Egyptian spice blend made with roasted nuts and aromatic spices. It is available from Middle-Eastern food stores, specialty spice stores and some supermarkets.

eggplant also known as aubergine.

fennel also known as finocchio or anise; a white to very pale green-white, firm, crisp, roundish vegetable about 8-12cm in diameter. The bulb has a slightly sweet, anise flavour but the leaves have a much stronger taste. Also the name of dried seeds having a licorice flavour.

fish fillets, firm white blue eye, bream, flathead, swordfish, ling, whiting, jewfish, snapper or sea perch are all good choices. Check for small pieces of bone and use tweezers to remove them.

five-spice powder also known as chinese five-spice; a fragrant mixture of ground cinnamon, cloves, star anise, sichuan pepper and fennel seeds.

flour

plain a general all-purpose wheat flour.

self-raising plain flour sifted with baking powder in the proportion of 1 cup flour to 2 teaspoons baking powder.

galangal a rhizome with a hot ginger-citrusy flavour; used similarly to ginger and garlic as a seasoning or an ingredient.

kaffir lime leaves also known as bai magrood. Aromatic leaves of a citrus tree; two glossy dark green leaves joined end to end, forming a rounded hourglass shape. A strip of fresh lime peel may be substituted for each kaffir lime leaf.

kecap manis see sauces, soy.

kumara the Polynesian name of an orange-fleshed sweet potato often confused with yam.

lebanese cucumber short, slender and thin-skinned. Probably the most popular variety because of its tender, edible skin, tiny, yielding seeds and sweet, fresh flavoursome taste.

lemon grass a tall, clumping, lemon-smelling and -tasting, sharp-edged grass; the white part of the stem is used, finely chopped, in cooking.

lentils (red, brown, yellow) dried pulses often identified by and named after their colour; also known as dhal.

mayonnaise we use whole-egg mayonnaise in our recipes.

mesclun a salad mix or gourmet salad mix with a mixture of assorted young lettuce and other green leaves, including baby spinach leaves, mizuna and curly endive.

mince also known as ground meat.

mirin a Japanese champagne-coloured cooking wine; made of glutinous rice and alcohol and used expressly for cooking. Should not be confused with sake.

mushrooms

enoki clumps of long, spaghetti-like stems with tiny, snowy white caps.

flat large, flat mushrooms with a rich earthy flavour. They are sometimes misnamed field mushrooms, which are wild mushrooms.

oyster also known as abalone; grey-white mushroom shaped like a fan. Prized for their smooth texture and subtle, oyster-like flavour.

shiitake when fresh are also known as chinese black, forest or golden oak mushrooms; although cultivated, they are large and meaty and have the earthiness and taste of wild mushrooms. When dried, they are known as donko or dried chinese mushrooms; rehydrate before use.

swiss brown also known as cremini or roman mushrooms; are light brown mushrooms with a full-bodied flavour.

mustard seeds are available in black, brown or yellow varieties. They are available from major supermarkets and health-food shops.

noodles

bean thread vermicelli made from mung bean flour. Fine, delicate noodles also known as wun sen, cellophane or glass noodles (because they are transparent when cooked). Available dried in various-sized bundles. Must be soaked to soften before use.

dried rice stick see rice vermicelli, dried (below).

egg, fresh also known as ba mee or yellow noodles. Made from wheat flour and eggs. Range in size from very fine strands to wide, thick spaghetti-like pieces as thick as a shoelace.

hokkien also known as stir-fry noodles; fresh wheat noodles resembling thick, yellow-brown spaghetti needing no pre-cooking.

ramen, fresh comes in various shapes and lengths. They may be fat, thin or even ribbon-like, as well as straight or wrinkled. While more often sold dried, fresh ramen is available from some Asian food stores. Substitute with reconstituted dried noodles.

rice vermicelli, dried very fine noodles made from rice flour and water, vermicelli is often compressed into blocks and dried. Before using, soak in boiling water until tender.

soba a thin spaghetti-like pale brown noodle from Japan; made from buckwheat and varying proportions of wheat flour.

onions

green also known as scallion or, incorrectly, shallot; an immature onion picked before the bulb has formed. Has a long, bright-green edible stalk.

red also known as spanish, red spanish or bermuda onion; a sweet-flavoured, large, purple-red onion.

shallots also called french shallots, golden shallots or eschalots; small, brown-skinned, elongated members of the onion family.

spring have small white bulbs and long, narrow, green-leafed tops.

pak choy similar to baby buk choy, except the stem is a very pale green, rather than white, and the top is less leafy.

pappadums are dried cracker-like wafers made from lentil and rice flours, if uncooked, they must be reconstituted before they are eaten. We do this the low-fat way, giving them a burst in a microwave oven, but they are usually deep-fried to make them puff and double in size.

paprika ground, dried, sweet red capsicum (bell pepper); there are many types available, including sweet, hot, mild and smoked.

parsley, flat-leaf also known as continental or italian parsley.

pasta

farfalle is a short, rather sturdy butterfly-shaped pasta that is also known as 'bow-ties'.

fusilli also known as 'corkscrews'. Dried spiral-shaped pasta.

rigatoni a form of tube-shaped pasta. it is larger than penne and is usually ridged, the end doesn't terminate at an angle, like penne does.

peppercorns

pink dried berry from a type of rose plant grown in Madagascar, usually sold packed in brine; they possess a distinctive pungently sweet taste.

sichuan also known as chinese pepper. Small, red-brown aromatic seeds resembling black peppercorns; they have a peppery-lemon flavour.

pitta also known as lebanese bread.

pizza bases pre-packaged for home-made pizzas. They come in a variety of sizes (snack or family) and thicknesses (thin and crispy or thick).

polenta also known as cornmeal; a flour-like cereal made of ground corn (maize). Also the name of the dish made from it.

prawn also known as shrimp.

preserved lemon rind a North African specialty; lemons are quartered and preserved in salt and lemon juice or water. To use, remove and discard pulp, squeeze juice from rind, rinse rind well; slice thinly. Once opened, store under refrigeration.

prosciutto a kind of unsmoked italian ham; salted, air-cured and aged.

rice

basmati a white, fragrant long-grained rice. Wash several times before cooking.

jasmine fragrant long-grained rice; white rice can be substituted, but will not taste the same.

rocket also known as arugula, rugula and rucola; a peppery-tasting green leaf. Baby rocket leaves are both smaller and less peppery.

sake made from fermented rice. If sake is unavailable, dry sherry, vermouth or brandy can be substituted. Cooking sake (containing salt) is also available.

sambal oelek (also ulek or olek) Indonesian in origin; a salty paste made from ground chillies and vinegar. Found in supermarkets and Asian food stores.

sauces

black bean a Chinese sauce made from fermented soya beans, spices, water and wheat flour.

char siu a Chinese barbecue sauce made from sugar, water, salt, fermented soya bean paste, honey, soy sauce, malt syrup and spices. It can be found at most supermarkets.

fish also called nam pla or nuoc nam; made from pulverised salted fermented fish, most often anchovies. Has a pungent smell and strong taste, so use sparingly.

hoisin a thick, sweet and spicy Chinese paste made from salted fermented soya beans, onions and garlic.

oyster Asian in origin, this rich, brown sauce is made from oysters and their brine, cooked with salt and soy sauce, and thickened with starches.

plum a thick, sweet and sour dipping sauce made from plums, vinegar, sugar, chillies and spices.

soy made from fermented soya beans. Several variations are available in most supermarkets and Asian food stores. We use japanese soy sauce unless otherwise indicated. It is the best table soy and the one to choose if you only want one type.

dark soy deep brown, almost black in colour; rich, with a thicker consistency than other types. Pungent but not that salty.

japanese soy an all-purpose low-sodium soy sauce made with more wheat content than its Chinese counterparts.

kecap manis (ketjap manis); a thick soy sauce with added sugar and spices. The sweetness is derived from the addition of molasses or palm sugar.

light soy a fairly thin, pale but salty tasting sauce; used in dishes in which the natural colour of the ingredients is to be maintained. Do not confuse with salt-reduced or low-sodium soy sauces.

sweet chilli a mild sauce made from red chillies, sugar, garlic and vinegar.

silver beet also known as swiss chard; mistakenly called spinach.

snow peas also called mange tout (eat all). Snow pea tendrils, the growing shoots of the plant, are also available at greengrocers.

snow pea sprouts are the tender new growths of snow peas.

spinach also known as english spinach and, incorrectly, silver beet.

sugar

brown very soft, finely granulated sugar retaining molasses for its characteristic colour and flavour.

caster also known as superfine or finely granulated table sugar.

white a coarsely granulated table sugar, also known as crystal sugar.

sugar snap peas are also known as honey snap peas; fresh small peas that can be eaten whole, pod and all, similarly to snow peas.

sumac a purple-red, astringent spice ground from berries growing on shrubs flourishing wild around the Mediterranean; adds a tart, lemony flavour to food. Available from spice shops and major supermarkets.

tahini a rich, sesame-seed paste, used in most Middle-Eastern cuisines.

turmeric related to ginger; adds a golden-yellow colour to food.

vinegar

balsamic originally from Modena, Italy, there are now many balsamic vinegars on the market ranging in pungency and quality depending on how long they have been aged. Is a deep rich brown colour and has a sweet and sour flavour. Quality can be determined up to a point by price; use the most expensive sparingly.

red wine based on fermented red wine.

rice a colourless vinegar made from fermented rice, sugar and salt. also known as seasoned rice vinegar.

white made from spirit of cane sugar.

white wine made from white wine.

vietnamese mint not a mint at all, but a pungent and peppery narrow-leafed member of the buckwheat family.

water chestnut resembles a chestnut in appearance, hence the English name. They are small brown tubers with a crisp, white, nutty-tasting flesh. Their crunchy texture is best experienced fresh, however, canned water chestnuts are more easily obtained and can be kept for about a month, once opened, under refrigeration.

white miso paste Japan's famous bean paste made from fermented soya beans and rice, rye or barley. It varies in colour, texture and saltiness.

watercress one of the cress family, a large group of peppery greens. Highly perishable, so must be used as soon as possible after purchase.

wombok also known as napa, peking or chinese cabbage or petsai. Elongated in shape with pale green, crinkly leaves. This is the most common cabbage in South-East Asian cooking.

conversion chart

measures

One Australian metric measuring cup holds approximately 250ml; one Australian metric tablespoon holds 20ml; one Australian metric teaspoon holds 5ml. The difference between one country's measuring cups and another's is within a two- or three-teaspoon variance, and will not affect your cooking results. North America, New Zealand and the United Kingdom use a 15ml tablespoon.

All cup and spoon measurements are level. The most accurate way of measuring dry ingredients is to weigh them. When measuring liquids, use a clear glass or plastic jug with the metric markings.

The imperial measurements used in these recipes are approximate only. Measurements for cake pans are approximate only. Using same-shaped cake pans of a similar size should not affect the outcome of your baking. We measure the inside top of the cake pan to determine sizes.

We use large eggs with an average weight of 60g.

dry measures

metric	imperial
15g	½oz
30g	1oz
60g	2oz
90g	3oz
125g	4oz (¼lb)
155g	5oz
185g	6oz
220g	7oz
250g	8oz (½lb)
280g	9oz
315g	10oz
345g	11oz
375g	12oz (¾lb)
410g	13oz
440g	14oz
470g	15oz
500g	16oz (1lb)
750g	24oz (1½lb)
1kg	32oz (2lb)

liquid measures

metric	imperial
30ml	1 fluid oz
60ml	2 fluid oz
100ml	3 fluid oz
125ml	4 fluid oz
150ml	5 fluid oz
190ml	6 fluid oz
250ml	8 fluid oz
300ml	10 fluid oz
500ml	16 fluid oz
600ml	20 fluid oz
1000ml (1 litre)	1¾ pints

length measures

metric	imperial
3mm	⅛in
6mm	¼in
1cm	½in
2cm	¾in
2.5cm	1in
5cm	2in
6cm	2½in
8cm	3in
10cm	4in
13cm	5in
15cm	6in
18cm	7in
20cm	8in
22cm	9in
25cm	10in
28cm	11in
30cm	12in (1ft)

oven temperatures

The oven temperatures in this book are for conventional ovens; if you have a fan-forced oven, decrease the temperature by 10-20 degrees.

	°C (CELSIUS)	°F (FAHRENHEIT)
Very slow	120	250
Slow	150	300
Moderately slow	160	325
Moderate	180	350
Moderately hot	200	400
Hot	220	425
Very hot	240	475

index